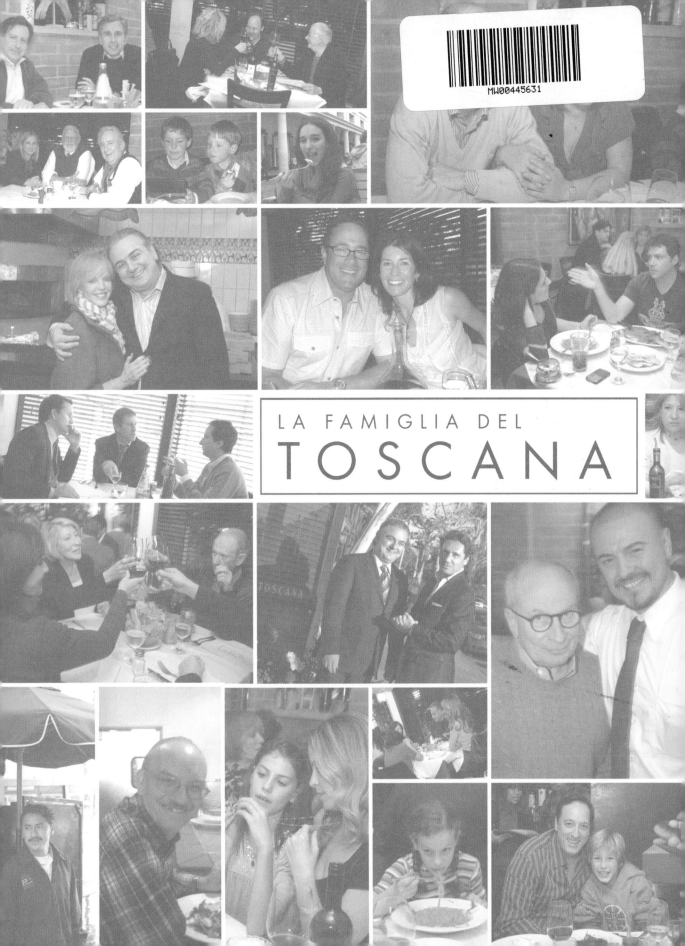

LA FAMIGLIA DEL
TOSCANA

Delicious warm wishes,
from our family to yours,

Kathie Gordon

2014

T O S C A N A

Text © Kathie Gordon and James O. Fraioli
Recipes © Killer Pizza Enterprises, Inc.
Cover & Food Photography © 2009 Jessica Nicosia-Nadler
Lifestyle Photography © 2009 Meagan Szasz
Food Styling @ 2009 Amy Gordon

Published in the United States by
Killer Pizza Enterprises, Inc.
11812 San Vicente Blvd.
Los Angeles, California, 90049
www.toscanabrentwood.com

ISBN-13: 978-0-615-30846-3
ISBN-10: 0-615-30846-5

Printed and bound in China through Globalink

Designed by theBookDesigners
www.bookdesigners.com

10 9 8 7 6 5 4 3 2 1

Library of Congress Cataloging-in-Publication data available.

TOSCANA

Simple Authentic Italian Recipes

From our family to yours

CELEBRATING
20
YEARS

KATHIE & AMY GORDON

WITH JAMES O. FRAIOLI

FOOD PHOTOGRAPHY BY JESSICA NICOSIA-NADLER
LIFESTYLE PHOTOGRAPHY BY MEAGAN SZASZ

KILLER PIZZA ENTERPRISES, INC. *Los Angeles*

TO ALL OF OUR *FAMIGLIE* WHO HAVE ENCOURAGED, INSPIRED, WORKED FOR US, AND CHALLENGED US TO KEEP *TOSCANA* TRUE TO ITS ROOTS. IT IS THESE FAMILIES WHO HAVE HELPED FULFILL OUR DREAMS OF FEEDING THE BODIES AND NURTURING THE SOULS OF OUR FRIENDS AND NEIGHBORS FOR THE PAST TWENTY YEARS. *TOSCANA* WOULD NOT BE WITHOUT YOU.

CONTENTS

PREFACE

Driving down San Vicente Boulevard in the early 1990s, we said to ourselves, "You know, we should try that restaurant one day." Fifteen hundred dinners later, we are proud to say we love *Toscana* more than ever. We have thirty favorite dishes, and that's a major reason why we eat at *Toscana* as many nights a week as possible.

But what makes the restaurant so successful are the people. When we walk into *Toscana*, it is like walking into the home of close friends. We've known much of the staff for many years, particularly Francesco, Antonio, Mark, Antonella, and Alberto. They are like our extended family. They make every dinner feel like a celebration. It's frightening to think of what it would be like without our "Big T."

So Cheers, Ciao, Mazel Tov, and a toast in a hundred languages to you all … and a thousand 'thank you's!

AL & LINDA MICHAELS

Al Michaels has been a prime network television sportscaster for more than three decades.

FOREWORD

Last week I ate at *Toscana* three times — once for lunch and twice for dinner. I chose *Toscana* because it's perfect for any occasion: friends, business, or a romantic evening out. The reason it's perfect is the amazing food and the service.

The food is healthy, clean, and special, but seasoned in such a unique way. The taste sensations are remarkable. I love the chicken, veal, artichoke salad, and the salmon with arugula and tomatoes... all the fish dishes. I realize every dish I have there is my favorite.

From the minute Francesco greets me with his warm smile, the entire staff makes me feel so welcome — like I'm eating in my own home. It all starts at the top, with Mike and Kathie Gordon, who opened the restaurant with a love of people, a love of food, and integrity in everything they do.

Writing this has made me hungry, and I'm now rushing off to another great meal at *Toscana*.

SHERRY LANSING
Philanthropist and former CEO of Paramount Pictures

I am running one morning with the owner of the building I want to rent for the restaurant. He is an avid climber who enjoys sharing stories of his mountainous treks, especially his successful climb of Mt. Everest. His eyes illuminate when he tells me what he enjoys most about the sport is overcoming the inherent risks and defeating what many believe to be the impossible. So, when he stops to ask me why in the world I want to open a restaurant, I smile and reply, "Why did you want to climb Everest?"

MIKE GORDON
President & Co-founder

TOSCANA

THE
TOSCANA
STORY

OUR DREAMS ARE REALIZED

It might seem the dream of *Toscana* was brought to life in the mid-1980s when Mike received a unique birthday gift: spend the day with Wolfgang Puck.

But in reality, the seed was planted by Mike's father, Bobby Gordon. Bobby loved food and he loved to eat. He passed that passion on to Mike, who took it a step further and learned to cook. Keeping it in the family, Mike passed his passion on to his son, *Toscana* co-owner Andy. Today his son, and Mike's grandson, fifteen-year-old Danny Gordon, fills his summer hours making pizzas at the restaurant.

I cannot minimize that day with Wolfgang, however, for while strolling through a farmers market with him, learning how to select the finest of fresh ingredients, and ending that memorable day crafting gourmet pizza with his friend at the illustrious *Spago*, Mike had an epiphany. Let's open a pizza take-out restaurant where customers could come in, select their own fresh, creative toppings, and leave with a custom-made pizza. Realizing our pizza dream became more reality than fantasy, as I had just completed a management program at the University of Southern California, and I quickly enrolled in restaurant development classes at UCLA. Meanwhile Mike picked the brain of chef/creator of *California Pizza Kitchen's* original menu. Although our pizza venture never came to be, we created the building blocks which would eventually lead to *Toscana*.

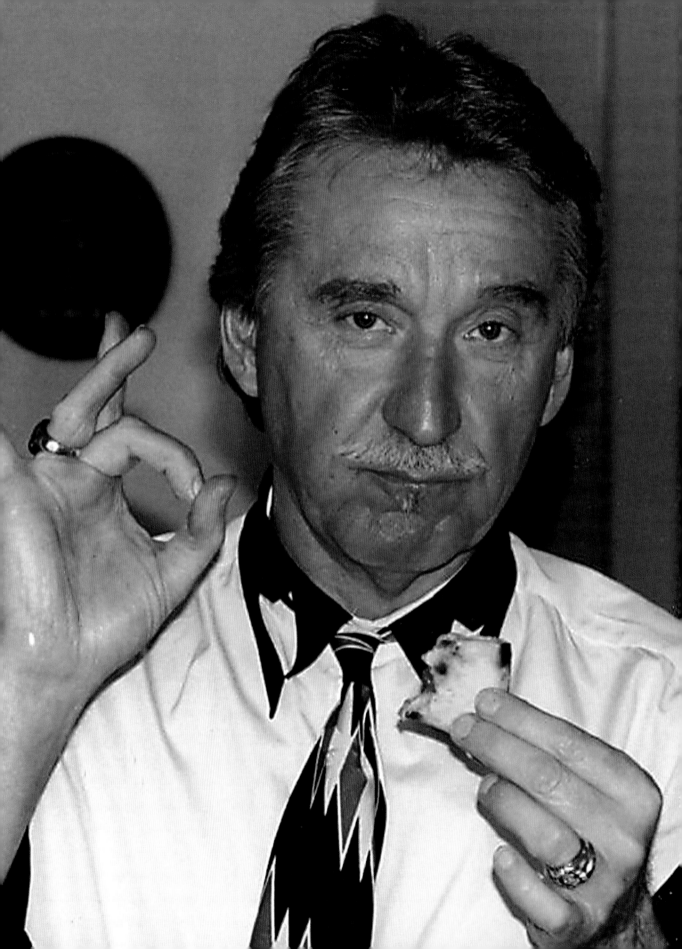

Along our way, Mike's client and our good friend Doc Severinsen (best known as the bandleader for Johnny Carson for more than 25 years) invited us to dinner at the former *Il Giardino* in Beverly Hills. There he introduced us to delicious Northern Italian dishes such as *carpaccio con parmigiano, penne ai gamberi, spaghetti alla bottarga*, grilled lamb chops with amazing roasted rosemary potatoes, and Executive Chef Agostino Sciandri – an authentic Tuscan in every sense of the word. In conversing with the chef, we all agreed there was something to say about having a love affair with traditional Tuscan cooking.

WE WANTED OUR GUESTS TO HAVE AN "AT HOME" FEELING WHERE THEY COULD LINGER, WHETHER OVER THEIR LAST GLASS OF WINE, CHOSEN FROM OUR IMPRESSIVE CALIFORNIA AND ITALIAN WINE LIST, OR OVER ANY ONE OF OUR TASTY HOMEMADE *DOLCI*.

When we returned home and reflected on the evening and the new taste sensations we had experienced, we redefined our mission: Create a Northern Italian trattoria in our own neighborhood where our friends and family could come together to eat this simple, yet delicious food. Our goal was set to create a warm and inviting, yet entertaining environment. We wanted our guests to have an "at home" feeling where they could linger, whether over their last glass of wine, chosen from our impressive California and Italian wine list, or over any one of our tasty homemade *dolci*. We also wanted our staff to be dedicated, welcoming employees who shared one common goal: Make every guest's dining experience the best it could be.

Our knowledge of the restaurant business was pretty much limited to our experience as diners. Notwithstanding our naivete, we forged ahead completing our business plan and looking for that one perfect location. It wasn't long before Mike stumbled upon a medical building for lease on the corner of San Vicente Boulevard and Darlington in Brentwood. The owner, Dan Emmett, who was one of Mike's occasional running partners, listened to Mike's convincing argument that Brentwood needed an authentic Italian restaurant rather than the frozen yogurt shop that happened to be competing for the same space. Dan agreed.

Upon signing the lease in 1988, Mike forfeited his deposit to John Wooden's Basketball Camp and we jumped on a plane destined for Tuscany with notepad and camera in hand. We spent two diligent weeks at every Italian *ristorante* and *trattoria* we found, learning everything we could, from the specials of the day to the color of the floor tiles in the restrooms. We were determined to bring the warmth of Italy back home with us.

Once home, Mike took my business plan and injected his professional business acumen and well thought out financial projections, and began making presentations to investors and bankers. Capitalizing on his myriad of connections from his business management firm, Mike appealed to Doc Severinsen and various other clients, along with many family members and friends. Everyone, it seemed, wanted to contribute to our dream, and soon Mike had raised the necessary funding needed to launch *Toscana*.

> BUT WE CLUNG TOGETHER, WORKED HARD, AND MANAGED TO STAY OUR COURSE, WEATHERING STORMS AND SURVIVING IN A CITY KNOWN FOR ITS RESTAURANT MORTALITY.

With our selected location sitting vacant and idle, we teamed up with a local architect to explore our ideas of designing an authentic Tuscan trattoria emphasizing the rustic nature and simplicity of Italy. Unfortunately the architect, not really grasping our concept, tried moving us into a very modern direction, whereupon we decided to complete the design ourselves with the help of Carol Zuckerman. We installed rich, hardwood floors in the seating area, old brick and mosaic tiles along the walls, and octagon-and diamond-shaped terra cotta tiles in the entry – a stark contrast to the new brick and glass exterior of the building. We also brought in a solid oak table with a nicked, paint-chipped surface that seats eight to twelve, which we call our *tavola della famiglia,* or Family Table. To this day, the table continues to be the most requested sitting area for dinner parties.

As 1988 came to a close, we invited Chef Agostino to run *Toscana's* kitchen and front of the house. Although he didn't love the idea of pizza in a trattoria, he was enthusiastic to

design the kitchen, create the menu, and lead the staff with his years of experience. More importantly, he taught us how to enjoy food—and life—in the traditional Italian way. Eager to get started and contribute to our success, I focused on the early administrative responsibilities while tackling marketing and promotional duties. Mike, of course, focused on the financial aspects of running a restaurant from his office two blocks away.

We have to admit, having never owned a restaurant before, at times we found ourselves losing sight of the romance. Focusing on the fun, creative elements like picking out linens, silverware, and art-work were now overshadowed with decisions about computers, alarm and phone systems, inventory software, and all the other necessary business details. Although, as exhausting as we remember it, *Toscana* flourished from the moment we opened the doors. And this is where

the essence of family took hold in *Toscana's* life. Mike, and myself, Agostino and his family, Hugo Vasquez and his three brothers, all of whom were with us when we opened our doors, formed the core of *Toscana's* spirit. Families hold each other together, and along with the help of other good people, many of whom are still with us today, our business grew. In spite of the doubters among our critics, we paid back all of our investors within the first eighteen months of business. Like climbing a mountain, every day brought new challenges. But we clung together, worked hard, and managed to stay our course, weathering storms and surviving in a city known for its restaurant mortality.

In 2000, as the world rang in the new millennium and we celebrated our eleventh anniversary, we embraced Mike's son, Andy, and his wife, Amy, as our new partners and co-owners, thereby enriching *la famiglia del Toscana*. Andy took charge of the wine list, turning the *Toscana* cellar into a carefully balanced, award-winning, world-class venue. Amy raised our décor and physical appearance to the delight of our new generation of customers, adding touches of class and style to our cherished trattoria. We also welcomed a new General Manager/Managing partner, Francesco Greco, who brought an exuberance and vitality which energized our staff and warmed the hearts of our customers. Together, Andy, Amy, and Francesco have become our eyes toward the future.

FOR ALL OF YOU, OUR EXTENDED *FAMIGLIA*, THIS COOKBOOK IS NOT ONLY A COLLECTION OF OUR MOST CHERISHED, AUTHENTIC DISHES THAT ARE SIMPLE AND EASY TO MAKE AT HOME, BUT A TRIBUTE TO *TOSCANA'S* TWENTY YEARS OF SUCCESS.

Among other changes we encouraged Hugo Vasquez, already noted as a *Toscana* original, to climb his own mountain, to grow with us from a fledgling busser to our current Executive Chef, our proud "*Capocuoco.*" Chef Hugo, who was 18 when he helped open *Toscana's* doors, is now 38 and admits he is never afraid of experimenting, and we appreciate his sense of culinary adventure in taking our Tuscan cuisine to new heights. Come to *Toscana* one night and you will see and taste what I'm talking about. From his fresh grilled calamari or warm lobster salad, to an extraordinary *ossobuco*, lamb shank, or a moist and utterly impeccable John Dory with lemon and capers, you will find the lunch and evening specials are just as intoxicating as the pasta, risotto, and wood-fired pizzas. Just like Italy!

For all of you, our extended *famiglia*, this cookbook is not only a collection of our most cherished, authentic dishes that are simple and easy to make at home, but a tribute to *Toscana's* twenty years of success. We thank everyone who has shared a table with us and to those who will visit and support us in the years ahead. We feel we have created a wonderful neighborhood hangout for visitors from around the world and locals alike. We see it as a place that is solid, snug, and intimate, yet electrifying with a wonderfully controlled chaos. We also believe it is our customers who create the hive of activity that makes *Toscana* what it is today. Despite the infinite numbers of restaurants that exist in the greater Los Angeles area, our guests tell us they come to us not only for the delicious food and decadent desserts, but because they want to experience a special place that feels like family and to which they are comfortable bringing their friends home to. The very same place we envisioned when we opened our doors twenty years ago.

KATHIE GORDON
Co-founder & Co-owner
From our family to yours, Buon Appetito!

OUR DREAMS FOR THE FUTURE

Toscana is what it set out to be—a locals' place for great food, communal atmosphere, and a warm feeling of being in a small Italian trattoria. After twenty years, it's hard to imagine how to make something so wonderful and perfect even better. From the time Mike and Kathie took the plunge and converted an old drugstore into their dream Italian destination in Brentwood, *Toscana* has adapted to the changing times very slowly as to not disrupt its consistent perfection. Sure, we re-stained the floors, added softer lighting, and tried to quiet down the dining room, but our real adaptation had to do with maintaining our quality of food and friendly approach to our clients each and every day, while introducing seasonal specials, a world-class, *Wine Spectator Award*-winning wine list, and the establishment of our wine cellar private dining room.

AS ENTHUSIASTIC ITALOPHILES WE TOO WOULD LOVE TO BRING ALIVE OUR MEMORIES OF EVENINGS WE HAVE HAD IN ITALY GAZING OVER THE ARNO, THE ITALIAN RIVIERA, OR THE GUIDECCA WHILE SIPPING A FAVORITE ITALIAN COCKTAIL AND DINING ON CLASSIC TUSCAN CUISINE.

As we look into the future, we will continue to embrace the essence of family as well as the traditions established by Mike and Kathie. But, as the younger generation, we can't help but be impelled to embellish and expand their original ideas and create new ones of our own. As enthusiastic Italophiles we too would love to bring alive our memories of evenings we have had in Italy gazing over the Arno, the Italian Riviera, or the Guidecca while sipping a favorite Italian cocktail and dining on classic Tuscan cuisine. We have inspirations that we hope to introduce in the not-too-distant future to all of our long-time customers along with the new ones of our generation.

We have been so honored and proud to be part of *Toscana* over the last ten years since we joined Mike and Kathie as partners. Francesco, our adopted brother, along with our dedicated team of twenty years including Hugo, Mark, Antonio, and Aberto, will continue to make all of you feel warm and welcome every time you visit.

Thanks to all of you, our *clienti*, for your patronage and support.

ANDY & AMY GORDON
Co-owners
Grazie e lunga vita al Toscana

MY REFLECTIONS

I had heard of *Toscana* since my early days in the restaurant business, but I had never been. One day I decided that I should walk in and begin a new venture, and as I entered through the glass door I had the chills. I felt at home – in Italy, somewhere in Panzano, Greve, or Viareggio. "*Che bello*, how wonderful," I thought, and fell in love with *Toscana*.

Throughout my first stint in the restaurant during the mid-90s I worked the floor and assistant managed. I have always savored the incredible, unique taste reflected in *Toscana's* ambience and its food, which defines the true essence of who we are. What Kathie and Mike had created transcended the usual casual eatery in that they assembled an exceptional and highly qualified professional staff that reveled in delivering the most deliciously simple, true Tuscan flavor, with its freshness and outstanding quality.

The Gordons invited me back at the end of 2000 to serve as General Manager and managing partner. This coincided with their new partnership with their children, Amy and Andy Gordon. Their continued support, whether intellectual, organizational, or financial, helped immensely in the overall décor of the restaurant and in exponentially improving our wine list. They absolutely complement Kathie and Mike's passion and make life for all of us very easy and fulfilled.

AS MIKE SAYS, "I WANT TO SEE TOSCANA BEYOND ME." I SAY ... "ME TOO!"

All the Gordons' encouragement and support prompted me to add perhaps the one ingredient missing in the mix; namely, More Love! True love for the only really significant factor in our business – the Customer. Because to do this job in the long run takes one quality: You have to enjoy people. In this respect, *Toscana* excels. We love our customers.

Finally, I want to sincerely thank Kathie and Mike for their vision and their heart, and Amy and Andy for their delicate but decisive touch and constant help. And, a million times over, I must thank all my wonderful colleagues whom everyday make *Toscana* the beautiful island on which we all live. And, as Mike says, "I want to see *Toscana* beyond me." I say ... "Me too!"

So, let's all have a nice glass of Super Tuscan and toast to *Toscana* forever.

FRANCESCO GRECO
General Manager, Managing Partner

In faith

Crisp. Fresh. Inviting. Three delicious words that define *Toscana's* signature salads. Co-founders Mike and Kathie Gordon proudly agree. "I'm a salad fanatic with a wife who grows vegetables at home, so freshness and quality are extremely important to me," says Mike. Kathie, whose favorite salad is *insalata di carciofi* (baby artichoke hearts with fennel and pecorino cheese), likes adding the word unique. "I enjoy unusual salads with

INSALATE

distinct flavors you can't find at other restaurants." Visit *Toscana* on any given day and you'll taste what the Gordons seek in tantalizing salads that will awaken your taste buds. From the simple *insalata di pomodori* (tomato) and *insalata di rucola* (arugula), to the ever-popular *insalata di aragosta* (lobster) and the surprising *insalata di farro* (salad with wheat berry), Toscana's elite culinary team, led by Executive Chef Hugo Vasquez, incorporates creativity, originality, and farmers market freshness into every salad, setting the bar for perfection.

TOSCANA'S SIGNATURE CONDIMENTI

These two dressings are simple to make and appear in many of Toscana's signature dishes.

CONDIMENTO ALL'ACETO BALSAMICO
BALSAMIC DRESSING
Makes 4 Servings

¼ cup olive oil
1½ tablespoons aged balsamic vinegar
¼ teaspoon salt
3 pinches black pepper
¼ teaspoon Dijon mustard
½ teaspoon fresh lemon juice

In a small bowl, whisk the oil, vinegar, salt, pepper, mustard, and lemon juice until well combined. Chill until ready to use.

CONDIMENTO AL LIMONE
LEMON DRESSING
Makes 4 Servings

¼ cup olive oil
1 tablespoon fresh lemon juice
¼ teaspoon salt
3 pinches black pepper

In a small bowl, whisk the oil, lemon juice, salt, and pepper until well combined. Chill until ready to use.

INSALATA DI RUCOLA
ARUGULA AND SLICES OF PARMESAN CHEESE
Serves 4

8 cups fresh arugula
1 medium vine-ripe tomato, sliced into 8 wedges
6 ounces fresh shaved parmesan cheese
½ cup balsamic dressing (see page 24)

Arrange the arugula on a serving plate or salad bowl. Place one wedge of tomato on each side of the salad. Top with shavings of parmesan cheese and finish with a drizzle of the balsamic dressing.

INSALATA TRICOLORE
THREE COLORED SALAD
Serves 4

1 cup arugula
4 cups radicchio
4 cups Belgian endive
2 vine-ripe tomatoes, cut into wedges
½ cup balsamic dressing (see page 24)
8 ounces fresh shaved parmesan cheese (optional)

On a serving plate, place the arugula, radicchio and Belgian endive separately, forming a three-color triangle (do not mix salads). Arrange the tomato wedges around the edge. Drizzle all the lettuce with the balsamic dressing and top with shaved parmesan cheese if desired.

INSALATA DI BARBABIETOLE

BEET SALAD

Serves 4

1 pound medium-size fresh red beets
Bowl of ice water
5 cups fresh baby mixed greens
½ cup balsamic dressing (see page 24)
2 fresh heirloom tomatoes
5 ounces fresh goat cheese, crumbled

Wash beets and add them to a boiling pot of water. Boil for about 1 hour 10 minutes, or until tender. Remove from heat, drain, and immediately submerge in a bowl of ice-water for about 5 minutes to stop the cooking process. When cool enough to handle, peel the beets and cut into julienne slices. In a separate bowl, toss the baby mixed greens with the balsamic dressing, and transfer to individual serving dishes. Slice the tomatoes into wedges and arrange around the edge of each salad. Top the salads with the julienne beets and crumbled goat cheese.

INSALATA DI POMODORI

TOMATO, CUCUMBER, AND RED ONION

Serves 4

6 medium vine-ripe tomatoes, sliced into ¼-inch thick rounds
1 English cucumber, peeled and thinly sliced into rounds
1 medium red onion, thinly sliced
½ cup balsamic dressing (see page 24)

Arrange the tomato slices in the center of a large plate. Arrange the cucumber rounds on top of the tomatoes. Top with the red onion slices and drizzle with the balsamic dressing.

MY WIFE AND I LOVE YOUR TOMATO, ONION, ANCHOVY, AND CUCUMBER SALAD WITH A LITTLE BALSAMIC VINEGAR. IT ALLOWS US TO ATTACK YOUR CRISPY PIZZA *MARGHERITA* AND *PENNE ARRABBIATA* GUILT FREE.

DAVID & BRYNN STEINBERG

INSALATA DI CARCIOFI
BABY ARTICHOKE SALAD
Serves 4

This dish is a *Toscana* original, and one of our most requested salads.

2 cups baby artichokes, thinly sliced
Bowl of ice water
½ cup fresh squeezed lemon juice
4 tablespoons fresh fava beans (or frozen)
1 fresh fennel bulb, thinly sliced (about ½ cup)
2 teaspoons salt
2 teaspoons black pepper
4 tablespoons walnuts, roasted and chopped
8 tablespoons extra virgin olive oil
Fresh shaved pecorino cheese (about 4 ounces)

Remove the outer leaves of the baby artichokes and thinly slice the chokes. Add the lemon juice to the water and soak the artichoke slices for a minimum of 1 hour to overnight. Next, prepare the fava beans by boiling them for three minutes until tender. Drain and cool the beans and remove the outer skins by hand. After draining the pre-soaked artichoke slices combine them in a medium-size bowl along with sliced fennel, cooked fava beans, salt, black pepper, and toasted walnuts. (Simply toast by adding walnuts to a pan over medium heat for no more than a moment or two.) Add the olive oil and toss well. Transfer to serving plates and top with fresh shavings of pecorino cheese and a drizzle of olive oil.

Chef's note: Artichokes oxidize, turning color once the cut edges are exposed to air. A soak in lemon water will prevent discoloration, as well as take away their bitterness.

THE FOOD IS RIDICULOUSLY GOOD, THE ATMOSPHERE IS WARM AND FRIENDLY, AND THE PERSONNEL IS RELATIVELY ATTRACTIVE. TRY THE *CARCIOFI* SALAD WITH THE FAVA BEANS. YOU WON'T BE UNHAPPY.

ROB REINER

INSALATA DI FARRO

FARRO SALAD

Serves 4

1½ cups farro
Bowl of ice water
½ cup arugula
1 finely chopped cucumber, seeds removed
2 plum tomatoes, finely chopped with seeds removed
1 teaspoon salt
¼ teaspoon black pepper
1½ tablespoons red wine vinegar
3 tablespoons extra virgin olive oil
4 cups baby mixed greens
4 tablespoons balsamic dressing (see page 24)
10 ounces fresh shaved parmesan cheese

Prepare the *farro* by washing under cold water and then soaking it overnight in water. Drain the *farro* and add to a boiling pot of unsalted water for 25 minutes. Remove from heat and immediately transfer to an ice bath (bowl of cold water and ice) to stop cooking process. When cold, drain the *farro* and set aside. Next, combine the arugula, cucumber, and tomato in a bowl. Add the cooked *farro*, salt, pepper, red wine vinegar, and olive oil. Toss well. Arrange the mixed greens on one side of each serving dish. Drizzle with the balsamic dressing. On the other side of the plate, arrange the *farro* salad and top both salads with fresh shaved parmesan cheese before serving.

Chef's note: Farro is an old-world wheat variety commonly found in Italy. In the U.S. *farro* can be found in most Italian markets, grocery stores, or ordered on the Internet. Wheat berries can be substituted for *farro*.

INSALATA DI FUNGHI SHIITAKE

SHIITAKE MUSHROOM SALAD

Serves 4

3 cups fresh shiitake mushrooms (stems removed)
2 tablespoons extra virgin olive oil
2 teaspoons salt
2 teaspoons black pepper
2 cups arugula, julienne
2 cups Belgian endive, julienne
2 cups radicchio, julienne
½ cup balsamic dressing (see page 24)
1 vine-ripe tomato, finely chopped with seeds removed
1 teaspoon chopped fresh Italian parsley

Clean the mushrooms and coat them with the olive oil, salt and pepper. On a hot kitchen grill or sauté pan, grill mushrooms on each side until tender (being careful not to burn them). Remove from heat and let cool. In a bowl combine the arugula, Belgian endive, and radicchio and toss with the balsamic dressing. Arrange salad mixture on a serving dish. Slice mushrooms in half and place on top of salad. Add the chopped tomato and sprinkle parsley around the edges.

INSALATA DI POLLO
GRILLED CHICKEN SALAD

Serves 1

1 large chicken breast (about 6 ounces), boneless and skinless
3 pinches salt
2 pinches black pepper
½ teaspoon olive oil
2 cups mixed baby greens
½ medium vine-ripe tomato, sliced
2 tablespoons balsamic dressing (see page 24)

Season the chicken breast with salt, pepper, and olive oil. Grill the chicken breast over a hot flame on an outdoor barbecue grill, or sauté in a pan over medium-high heat (about 5 minutes per side, until tender). Remove from grill and slice at an angle into thin medallions. Return to the grill to warm and ensure it is properly cooked through. Next, arrange the mixed baby greens on a serving plate. Place the tomato slices on one side of salad. Top with the chicken breast medallions and drizzle with balsamic dressing.

INSALATA DI GAMBERI
SAUTÉED SHRIMP SALAD

Serves 1

6 ounces (40/50 CT) fresh shrimp (about 12 pieces), peeled and deveined
2 pinches salt
2 pinches black pepper
½ teaspoon olive oil
2 tablespoons lemon dressing (see page 24)
2 cups fresh arugula
3 to 4 cherry tomatoes, halved
½ avocado, peeled and sliced

Wash the shrimp under cold water and pat dry with paper towel. Next, season the shrimp with salt, pepper, and olive oil. In a sauté pan, add shrimp and cook over medium-high heat, until tender (about 5 minutes). Remove pan from heat and add the lemon dressing. Toss well to coat the shrimp. Arrange the arugula on a serving plate and place the tomato halves and avocado slices around the edge. Top with the sautéed shrimp and pan juices.

THE PLACE IS LIKE A PRIVATE CLUB WHERE I HAVE A PERSONAL RELATIONSHIP WITH THE STAFF AS WELL AS THE REGULARS. A SPECIAL REMEMBRANCE IS THE NIGHT WE HOSTED OUR CLOSE FRIENDS MITT AND ANNE ROMNEY DURING THE HOLIDAYS JUST BEFORE HIS ANNOUNCEMENT OF HIS CANDIDACY FOR PRESIDENT. THE COMFORT OF THE ATMOSPHERE AND COURTESY OF THE STAFF ENABLED US TO ENJOY A WARM AND FUN EVENING.

TOM TELLEFSEN & STEPHANIE SPENCER

INSALATA DI CALAMARI
SAUTÉED CALAMARI SALAD

Serves 1

1 cup fresh baby calamari, tubes and tentacles (about 10 ounces), cleaned
2 pinches salt
2 pinches black pepper
½ teaspoon olive oil
2 tablespoons lemon dressing (see page 24)
1 tablespoon fresh Italian parsley, finely chopped
1 tablespoon freshly diced vine-ripe tomato
2 cups mixed baby greens
3 Belgian endive leaves

Wash the calamari under cold water and pat dry with paper towel. Slice the tubes in half and split open. Season the calamari with salt, pepper, and olive oil. In a sauté pan add calamari and cook over medium-high heat, until tender (about 5 minutes). Remove pan from heat and add the lemon dressing, Italian parsley, and tomato. Toss well to coat the calamari. Next, arrange the mixed baby greens on a serving plate. Place the Belgian endive leaves around the edge. Top with the sautéed calamari, parsley, tomato, and pan juices.

WHAT WE LOVE ABOUT *TOSCANA* IS THAT IT FEELS LIKE A FAMILY TRADITION—SUNDAY NITES—EARLY DINNER. CONGRATULATIONS FOR MAKING SUCH A WONDERFUL, CARING, AND DELICIOUS TRADITION AND THANK YOU! P.S. SEE YOU SUNDAY AT 6:00.

THE STACEY AND HENRY WINKLER FAMILY

ARAGOSTA LESSATA IN INSALATA
WARM LOBSTER SALAD

Serves 2

This salad makes 2 servings, utilizing all of the lobster meat.

1½ pound live Maine lobster
1 tablespoon extra virgin olive oil
1 garlic clove, smashed with a knife
1 cup Yukon gold potatoes, peeled and cubed
1 cup fresh zucchini, cubed
½ teaspoon salt
Pinch of pepper
6 leaves of Boston or butter lettuce
½ carrot, peeled and julienne for garnish
¼ cup lemon dressing (see page 24)

In a large pot, boil water and add salt if desired. Add the lobster and cook for 10 minutes per pound (add 2 minutes for each ¼ pound). Begin timing once the water returns to a boil. Remove lobster and let cool until easy to handle. Remove tail and claw meat and roughly chop.

Add olive oil to a large sauté pan over medium-high heat and add the garlic. Sauté garlic until golden and add the cubed potatoes, zucchini, salt, and pepper and cook for about 4 minutes. Add the lobster meat and toss well. Remove from heat and discard the garlic.

On each large serving plate, arrange 3 lettuce leaves in the center. Add the sautéed lobster (about ½ cup of lobster meat per serving) and vegetable mixture along with the pan juices. Top with the julienne carrot slices and drizzle with lemon dressing.

Chef's note: Unlike most Italian restaurants, *Toscana* prides itself on using very little garlic. In certain dishes throughout this book, the garlic is simply smashed with the side of a knife and added to release the wonderful aromatics before being removed when the dish is served.

Whether a lazy summer afternoon or a crisp winter evening, *Toscana's* light yet hearty soups are perfect comfort foods that warm the palate and rejuvenate the soul year 'round. Made with wonderfully fresh ingredients simmering over a kitchen flame, every delicious soup is served with a smile. Traditional favorites like Chef Hugo's *zuppa di ceci*, to the familiar and often requested *pasta e fagioli*,

ZUPPE E MINESTRE

soups can be prepared as the prelude to the main meal or served as a lunch or dinner special. Every once in a while, Chef Hugo breaks out with a rare soup, like *pappa al pomodoro*, an authentic Tuscan tomato soup with day-old bread, or *calamari in zimino*, a creative seafood soup with fresh squid and Swiss chard, first featured on the original *Toscana* menu. Visit *Toscana* and see which tasty soup is simmering on the stove.

ZUPPA DI FAGIOLI BORLOTTI

BORLOTTI BEAN SOUP

Serves 4

BEAN PREPARATION:

2½ cups dry borlotti beans

Water as needed to cover the beans

1 stalk celery, cut in half

1 stalk carrot, cut in half

1 half onion

Prepare the borlotti beans by soaking the beans overnight in water with the celery, carrot and, onion. Drain the beans, remove the veggies and add beans to a pot with fresh water. Cook over very low heat for about 1 hour until the beans are tender. Remove from heat, drain and set aside.

SOUP PREPARATION:

4 tablespoons extra virgin olive oil

1 teaspoon salt

6 ounces fresh Swiss chard, chopped

10 ounces fresh green cabbage, chopped

1 medium yellow onion, finely chopped

9 cups water

4 slices rustic Italian bread

½ cup fresh grated parmesan cheese

In a large sauce pan over medium-high heat add the olive oil. When hot, add the Swiss chard, cabbage, yellow onion, and salt. Cook for 7 to 10 minutes. Reduce the heat to low, add the cooked beans and 9 cups of water and let simmer for 20 minutes.

After simmering, top with the parmesan cheese and place pan in a preheated oven set on broil. When cheese is bubbly and golden, remove from heat.

Meanwhile toast the bread under the broiler until golden brown and transfer to individual serving bowls. Carefully divide the melted cheese and bean soup on top of each piece of toasted bread and serve immediately.

Chef's note: Borlotti beans are a plump variety of kidney bean, large in shape and pinkish brown in color with reddish-brown streaks. They are commonly used in Italian cooking because of their sweet and smooth, creamy texture. Borlotti beans are also high in protein and fiber. They are available in specialty food stores in jars, in which case one can skip the soaking and cooking process.

CALAMARI IN ZIMINO
CALAMARI AND SWISS CHARD SOUP

Serves 4

1 tablespoon extra virgin olive oil
2 garlic cloves, smashed
1 pound fresh baby calamari, tubes and tentacles,
*   cleaned, and tubes sliced in half*
½ teaspoon salt
½ cup dry white wine
¼ crushed red pepper (peperoncino)
7 ounces fresh Swiss chard
8 ounces fresh green peas (or frozen)
4 cups fresh tomato sauce (see page 103)
1 cup fresh fish stock (see page 79)
3 slices rustic Italian bread
3 garlic cloves, peeled and cut in half
½ tablespoon fresh chopped Italian parsley

Add the olive oil to a large sauce pan or small stock pot over medium-high heat. When hot, add the smashed garlic and sauté until soft and golden brown. Add the calamari, salt, wine, and red pepper, and stir for no more than 3 minutes. Remove the calamari and add the Swiss chard and peas to the pan, stirring occasionally. Add the tomato sauce and fish stock and continue to cook for 7 minutes until liquid is reduced. (Note: if using frozen peas, check now to see the peas are soft and tender.) Return the calamari to the pan and cook for an additional 3 minutes. Toast the bread slices under the broiler. When toasted, rub liberally with the garlic halves and cut toast slices in half. Remove the smashed garlic from the soup, and transfer the soup to individual serving bowls. Top with 1 or 2 pieces of toasted bread. Finish with a pinch of Italian parsley and a drizzle of olive oil.

ONE OF MY FAVORITE TOSCANA DISHES IS THE CALAMARI IN TOMATO SAUCE WITH GARLIC AND THE CHUNK OF BREAD THAT SOAKS UP THE DELICIOUS SAUCE. OF COURSE, I CAN'T REMEMBER WHAT IT'S CALLED!

ROSALIE SWEDLIN

PAPPA AL POMODORO
TOMATO AND BREAD SOUP
Serves 4

1 pound fresh vine-ripe tomatoes
3 tablespoons extra virgin olive oil, divided
½ tablespoon finely chopped yellow onion
1 cup fresh whole basil leaves, stems removed
3 slices fresh Italian bread
1 cup water
1 teaspoon salt
¼ teaspoon black pepper
1 cup chicken or vegetable stock

In a large pot of boiling water, add the tomatoes. Boil until soft and tender. Drain water and let tomatoes cool. When cool to the touch, remove the skin and seeds, and chop into 1-inch pieces.

In a large stainless steel pan over medium heat, add 1 tablespoon of olive oil. When hot, add the onions and basil and sauté until onions are translucent. Add the cooked tomatoes.

Next, remove the crust from the bread slices, lightly toast and cut into 1-inch pieces. Add to the pan. With a whisk, blend the tomato and bread into a smooth consistency, with the bread absorbing much of the liquid.

Add the water, and continue to whisk until absorbed. Add the salt, pepper, and stock. Reduce the heat to low and let simmer for about 15 minutes. Add the second tablespoon of olive oil. Continue to simmer for 10 minutes. Remove from heat, pull out about half of the basil leaves and transfer to individual serving bowls. Drizzle the remaining olive oil over the top. Optionally, garnish with lightly toasted bread cubes.

Chef's note: With this soup we prefer to use fresh tomatoes as often they are sweeter than canned tomatoes.

ZUPPA DI CECI

CHICKPEA SOUP

Serves 4

BEAN PREPARATION:

2 cups garbanzo beans
Water, as needed to soak and cook the beans
1 stalk celery, cut in half
1 stalk carrot, cut in half
½ onion, cut in half

Prepare the garbanzo beans by presoaking them overnight in water with celery, carrot, and onion (to flavor the water). Drain the beans, discard the veggies, and add beans to a pot with fresh water. Cook over very low heat for about 1 hour until the beans are tender. When done, set beans aside.

SOUP PREPARATION:

¼ cup extra virgin olive oil
1 carrot, finely chopped
2 stalks celery, finely chopped
2 tablespoons yellow onion, finely chopped
4 fresh sage leaves
12 cups water
½ teaspoon salt

In a saucepot over medium heat, add the extra virgin olive oil. When hot, add the carrots, celery, and onion. Cook until the onions are translucent. Add the sage leaves, cooked garbanzo beans, and the water. Reduce heat to low and allow to simmer for about 1 hour. Before serving, sprinkle with salt if desired.

Chef's note: Chickpeas are often known as garbanzo beans. They are widely available dried or in cans.

PASTA E FAGIOLI
PASTA AND BEAN SOUP
Serves 4

BEAN PREPARATION:

2 cups white cannellini beans
Water, as needed to soak and cook the beans
1 stalk celery, cut in half

1 carrot, cut in half
½ medium onion

Prepare the *cannellini* beans by presoaking them overnight in water with the celery, carrot, and onion (to flavor the water). Drain the beans, discard the veggies, and add them to a pot with fresh water. Cook over very low heat for about 1 hour until the beans are tender. Set aside.

SOUP PREPARATION:

2 ounces pancetta, roughly chopped
½ teaspoon minced garlic
2 fresh sage leaves

2 tablespoons chopped yellow onion
6 tablespoons extra virgin olive oil, divided

In a blender add the pancetta, garlic, sage, onion, and 4 tablespoons of extra virgin olive oil. Blend until well combined. In a saucepot over medium heat, add the remaining 2 tablespoons of olive oil. When hot add the blended mix. Stir and cook for about 4 minutes. Add the cooked cannellini beans and reduce heat to low. Allow to simmer for about 20 minutes.

PASTA PREPARATION:

½ cup cooked tubetti or macaroni pasta
4 quarts water
2 pinches salt

While soup mixture is simmering, prepare the pasta by boiling 4 quarts of water with the salt (optional). Add the pasta and stir, returning to a rapid boil. Cook uncovered according to package directions until al dente. When done, remove from heat and drain. To serve, divide the bean soup into individual serving bowls and top with equal amounts of the cooked pasta.

Chef's note: Toscana uses fresh *cannellini* beans for optimum flavor in many of its signature dishes as well as in many recipes in this cookbook. For convenience, we suggest you can use canned *cannellini* beans, just be sure to rinse them well under running water.

ZUPPA DI FAVE
FAVA BEAN SOUP
Serves 4

BEAN PREPARATION:

2½ cups dried yellow fava beans
(fresh, peeled beans can also be used)
Water, as needed to soak and cook the beans
1 carrot, cut in half
1 stalk celery, cut in half
½ onion

Prepare fava beans by soaking the beans overnight in water with the celery, carrot, and onion. Drain the beans, remove the veggies and add beans to a pot with fresh water. Cook over very low heat for about 1 hour until the beans are tender. Remove from heat, drain and set aside, reserving 4 cups of the cooking liquid.

SOUP PREPARATION:

4 tablespoons extra virgin olive oil
1½ teaspoons salt, divided
2 small finely chopped carrots
2 small finely chopped celery stalks
½ medium finely chopped onion

Heat a large saucepan or small stockpot over medium-high heat. Add the olive oil and when hot, add the carrot, celery, onion, cooked fava beans, and 1 teaspoon salt. Cook for 35 minutes.

Remove from heat and puree beans and vegetables along with the 4 cups of reserved cooking liquid in a blender or Cuisinart. Return puree back to pan over medium high heat, add the remaining teaspoon salt, and cook for 20 minutes. Transfer to individual serving bowls and finish with a drizzle of extra virgin olive oil.

MY DEFINITION OF A DREAM DINING EXPERIENCE STARTS WITH A HUG FROM FRANCESCO, A SHRUG FROM ALBERTO, FOLLOWED BY A SUBLIME PLATE OF PERFECTLY CRAFTED ITALIAN COOKING.

GREG COOTE

ZUPPA DI PESCE (CACCIUCCO)

SEAFOOD SOUP

Serves 4

4 tablespoons extra virgin olive oil, divided
2 garlic cloves, smashed
7 ounces fresh calamari, tubes and tentacles, with tubes sliced open
8 ounces live Manila clams
12 live New Zealand green mussels
8 ounces fresh shrimp, peeled and deveined
1 cup dry white wine
1 teaspoon salt
4 vine-ripe tomatoes, chopped with the seeds and soft center removed
2 cups fresh tomato sauce (see page 103)
2 cups fresh fish stock (see page 79), divided
8 ounces fresh Alaskan wild-caught salmon, cut into large cubes
8 ounces fresh sea bass (center cut), cut into large cubes
¼ teaspoon finely chopped fresh Italian parsley

In a large sauté pan over medium-high heat, add 3 tablespoons extra virgin olive oil. When hot, add the garlic, calamari, clams, mussels, and shrimp. Stir and cook for 2 minutes. Add the white wine and salt, and continue to cook 3 additional minutes.

Remove the calamari and shrimp and add the tomatoes, tomato sauce, and 1 cup fish stock. Let cook for about 5 minutes so liquids reduce. Stir occasionally.

Add the salmon and sea bass pieces and stop stirring. Add the remaining cup of fish stock.

Cover the pot and let simmer for 8 minutes. Return the calamari and shrimp to the pot, along with the remaining olive oil. Cook for another 2 minutes. Remove from heat, discard the garlic, and transfer to individual serving bowls. Arrange the clams, mussels, salmon, and sea bass on top, and finish with a sprinkle of the Italian parsley.

Dozens of different ingredients sourced locally and around the globe are used to make fresh, flavorful *Toscana* starters. Lunches often draw the *tuna carpaccio* and *burrata* crowd, and dinners are generally for pasta and meat lovers. But the one starter that's heralded by patrons and stands alone as the symbol of *Toscana* is the crisp and invitingly refreshing *pinzimonio*. Some call it an edible centerpiece that graces every dinner table at *Toscana*. Managing partner and GM Francesco Greco admits the *pinzimonio* brings back childhood memories. "When I was a boy growing up in Italy, my mother always stuffed carrots and celery into wine glasses and placed them around the dinner

ANTIPASTI

table," he says. "I never attended a meal where fresh vegetables weren't available." At *Toscana*, the *pinzimonio* is a table attraction, and can even be crafted to suit your personal tastes—should you happen to know the right people. Co-owner Amy Gordon notes the *pinzimonio* is not only visually striking but a fun addition, and a light and healthy alternative to a heavy basket of bread. While nibbling on *pinzimonio*, diners at *Toscana* can discover other tasty beginnings such as the always tempting *burrata*, which you won't find creamier than at *Toscana*, the *gamberi e fagioli*, another simple, flavorful, and healthy starter, or *insalata di mare*, a perfect appetizer for seafood lovers. For serious carnivores who have a natural passion for beef, the *tagliata alla Toscana* is a must—prepared with sliced dry-aged prime ribeye seared over a hot flame and crowned with creamy cannellini beans. There's no shortage of tantalizing starters to prepare the palate for what lies ahead.

PINZIMONIO
FRESH VEGETABLES WITH BALSAMIC DRESSING
Serves 4

Pinzimonio is our signature starter course, served on every dinner table. Fresh, chilled vegetables married with a tangy balsamic dressing not only revitalizes the taste buds, but truly defines *Toscana*. This unique Tuscan dish is an excellent start to the wonderful meal ahead."

—*Francesco Greco*

2 celery stalks, halved
4 slices of assorted green, red, and yellow bell pepper
1 large carrot, peeled and quartered
4 radishes
½ Belgian endive, sliced in half
Cubed ice
½ cup balsamic dressing (see page 24)

In a medium-size glass bowl, fill the bottom with ice. Arrange the fresh vegetables. Serve with a side of balsamic dressing for dipping.

Chef's note: Feel free to experiment with other fresh garden vegetables, such as broccoli and cauliflower tips or cherry tomatoes.

WHEN WE GO TO *TOSCANA* WE FEEL LIKE WE'RE IN A RUSTIC ITALIAN VILLAGE SURROUNDED BY OUR FRIENDS. THERE IS NOTHING LIKE THE CRUNCHY RAW VEGETABLES DIPPED IN VINAIGRETTE AND THE WARM *FOCACCIA* FRESH FROM THE OVEN, DRIZZLED WITH OLIVE OIL.

STEVEN & MICHELLE BROOKMAN

TAGLIATA ALLA TOSCANA
CON CANNELLINI

THINLY SLICED PRIME NEW YORK STEAK AND CANNELLINI BEANS

Serves 1

Like the salads, *Toscana* always prepares the starter courses in single servings. When making at home, feel free to double or triple the ingredient amounts to achieve additional servings.

4 ounces prime New York steak
1 teaspoon salt, divided
1 teaspoon black pepper, divided
½ teaspoon extra virgin olive oil
1 garlic clove, smashed
½ cup cooked white cannellini beans (see page 53 for cooking instructions)
½ teaspoon red wine vinegar
Pinch of fresh Italian parsley, finely chopped
Extra virgin olive oil, as needed

Season the steak with ½ teaspoon of salt and ½ teaspoon of pepper. On a hot outdoor barbecue, or stove-top grill, sear the steak for about 3 minutes on each side, until brown. Remove from the heat and let rest for about 5 minutes. With a sharp knife, thinly slice the steak and arrange on the bottom of a medium-size sauté pan. Add remaining ½ teaspoon of salt and pepper, and a drizzle of extra virgin olive oil. Set aside.

In a separate sauté pan, add ½ teaspoon of extra virgin olive oil, the smashed garlic clove, cooked white *cannellini* beans and red wine vinegar. Cook over medium-high heat for several minutes, remove and discard the garlic.

Next, finish the steak in a preheated 450 degree F oven until desired doneness. Remove from oven and arrange the steak slices on a serving plate. Top with the cooked *cannellini* beans, a pinch of Italian parsley and a drizzle of olive oil.

Chef's note: If you prefer using canned *cannellini* beans, make sure to rinse the beans well under cold running water before adding to the pan.

Twenty years ago Mike Gordon asked if I thought it was possible
to create a "trattoria-type" restaurant out of an unoccupied medical space in
Brentwood that had not only served as a pharmacy, but stood in an area not then
known for elaborate dining. I told him yes, and expressed that what the vacant
space needed was a large, distressed farm-style table to warm up the place and
make it feel "homey." In fact, I went on a search for the perfect table. And when I
strolled into the Mitchell Litt store, I quickly spotted the magical piece with all its
peeling paint and exposed planks.

I had that table trucked to *Toscana* where it served as the "family-style"
seating area for individuals dining by themselves. Soon, other individuals were

seated at the same table, and by the end of the night, total strangers who planned to dine alone were now toasting to new friendships made. Today the Family Table, as we call it, serves families needing a larger table with ample space while the individual diners now take a front row seat at the counter to observe all the chefs in action.

The other day, while having dinner at *Toscana*, I saw my table occupied by a family laughing and celebrating someone's birthday. It brought a smile to my face as the table, after all these years and although quite weathered, still looks as won-

BURRATA

CREAMY MOZZARELLA, BUTTER LETTUCE, AND FRESH TOMATO

Serves 1

½ medium vine-ripe tomato, sliced into thin wedges
1 cup Boston or butter lettuce leaves
3 slices fresh burrata cheese (about 6 ounces)
Pinch of salt
Pinch of black pepper
Drizzle of extra virgin olive oil

Arrange the tomato slices on a serving plate. Arrange the lettuce leaves between the tomato slices. Add the slices of *burrata* cheese in the center. Finish with a pinch of salt, pepper, and drizzle of extra virgin olive oil.

CARPACCIO DI TONNO

TUNA CARPACCIO

Serves 1

4 ounces fresh sushi-grade ahi tuna loin
¼ fresh lemon, juiced
1 tablespoon olive oil
pinch of salt
½ ounce fresh arugula
1 fresh Belgian endive leaf
½ fresh vine-ripe tomato, julienne

Place the ahi on top of a large sheet of plastic wrap, and place another large sheet on top. Using a kitchen mallet, pound the tuna piece until paper-thin. Transfer the pounded tuna piece to a serving dish.

Next, whisk the lemon juice, olive oil, and salt together in a small bowl and spoon over the tuna. Top with a small mound of arugula, an endive leaf, and a garnish of julienne tomato.

YOUR MOST PERFECT MEAL FOR ME IS CUSTOMIZED AND PERSONALIZED (AS ONLY *TOSCANA* DOES). THERE IS NOTHING BETTER IN LA—OR ROME.

BILL STADIEM
Food Critic & Author

GAMBERI CON FAGIOLI
SHRIMP WITH WHITE BEANS

Serves 1

1 tablespoon extra virgin olive oil
1 garlic clove, smashed
3 large prawns (or 4 to 5 ounces shrimp), shelled, deveined, and butterflied
2 pinches salt
2 pinches black pepper
2 splashes dry white wine (just a little less than ¼ cup)
1 cup cooked white cannellini beans (see page 53 for cooking instructions), or canned
Pinch of fresh Italian parsley, finely chopped

Heat olive oil in a sauté pan over medium-high heat. Add the garlic and cook until golden brown. Add the prawns (or shrimp), salt, pepper, and white wine. Cook for about 2 minutes.

Remove the prawns and add the cooked *cannellini* beans to the pan. Cook in the wine sauce for an additional 3 minutes. Return the prawns to the pan and cook for 2 more minutes. Remove from heat and discard the garlic. Transfer to a serving plate and garnish with a pinch of Italian parsley.

FOR ME IT'S ALL ABOUT RELATIONSHIPS. FOR MY LAST MEAL, I WANT TO BE AT *TOSCANA*. WHEN YOU COME IN, FRANCESCO EMBRACES YOU AND YOU FEEL YOU'RE PART OF THE FAMILY.

ARIANNA HUFFINGTON

MOLECHE AL FORNO
SOFT-SHELLED CRAB

Serves 1

2 soft-shelled crabs, cleaned and washed
½ teaspoon extra virgin olive oil
3 pinches salt
2 pinches black pepper
1 garlic clove, smashed
2 splashes dry white wine (just a little less than ¼ cup)
½ lemon, juiced
2 cups mixed baby greens
2 tablespoons vine-ripe tomato, diced
2 pinches fresh Italian parsley, finely chopped

Clean and wash the soft-shelled crab under running cold water by carefully lifting the top shell to remove the gills and innards. When finished pat dry with a paper towel. In a sauté pan, add the crab, extra virgin olive oil, salt, pepper, garlic, white wine, and lemon juice. Cook in a pre-heated 500 degrees F oven for 8 to 10 minutes. Remove from heat, discard the garlic, and set aside.

Next, add the mixed baby greens to a large serving plate and top with the diced tomato. Arrange the two crabs on top of the salad and spoon over the remaining pan juices. Garnish with the Italian parsley.

OUR TWO DAUGHTERS CAN BE CONVINCED TO DO ANYTHING IF THE REWARD IS DINNER AT TOSCANA.

DANA & MATT WALDEN

MELANZANE ALLA PARMIGIANA
EGGPLANT PARMESAN
Serves 1

TOMATO SAUCE
1 tablespoon chopped carrot
1 tablespoon chopped celery
1 tablespoon chopped yellow onion
3 fresh basil leaves
1 cup fresh tomato sauce (see page 103)
1 teaspoon olive oil

To prepare the tomato sauce, blend the carrot, celery, onion, and basil leaves into a puree. Add to a sauté pan with the tomato sauce and olive oil. Cook over low heat until ready to use.

EGGPLANT PREPARATION:
1 cup warm water
1½ cups all-purpose flour
2 pinches salt
2 pinches black pepper
1 tablespoon beer
⅓ fresh eggplant, peeled and sliced into 3 rounds, about ¼-inch thick
Vegetable oil, as needed for frying
¼ cup fresh grated parmesan cheese
¼ cup grated mozzarella cheese

Preheat oven to 500 degrees F. In a medium-size mixing bowl, add the warm water, flour, salt, pepper, and beer. Whisk into a batter. Set aside and let rest for about 15 minutes at room temperature.

Next, slice the eggplant into rounds, and prepare a pan with vegetable oil over medium-heat. When ready, dip each eggplant slice into the batter and fry in the oil until golden brown. Remove eggplant and drain on paper towel.

In a small ovenproof Au Gratin dish, spoon a layer of tomato sauce on the bottom. Add some parmesan cheese followed by 1 slice of eggplant. Continue the layering process of tomato sauce, parmesan cheese, and eggplant. Top with the mozzarella cheese and bake until the cheese is golden brown and bubbly. Remove and serve immediately.

CROSTINI
CROSTINI WITH ASSORTED TOPPINGS
Serves 4

LIVER SPREAD:

3 tablespoons extra virgin olive oil, divided

¼ teaspoon minced garlic

½ teaspoon capers

4 ounces chicken liver

¼ teaspoon salt

¼ teaspoon black pepper

Splash of white wine (about 1 tablespoon)

½ teaspoon butter, melted

Italian baguette, sliced and toasted

In a sauté pan over medium-high heat, add 2 tablespoons of the extra virgin olive oil. When hot, add the garlic, capers, chicken liver, salt, pepper, and white wine. Let cook for about 10 minutes, allowing wine to reduce. Remove from heat and let cool. When cool, add contents of the pan into a blender or Cuisinart. Add the butter and remaining tablespoon of olive oil, and blend until a smooth consistency is achieved. Spread the liver mixture on top of toasted baguette slices.

MIXED VEGETABLE SPREAD:

2 tablespoons extra virgin olive oil

¼ teaspoon fresh thyme

3 tablespoons finely chopped green pepper

3 tablespoons finely chopped red pepper

3 tablespoons finely chopped yellow pepper

3 tablespoons finely chopped zucchini

¼ teaspoon salt

¼ teaspoon black pepper

1 egg

1 tablespoon fresh grated parmesan cheese

In a sauté pan over medium-high heat, add the extra virgin olive oil. When hot, add the thyme and the chopped green, red, and yellow peppers and zucchini. Sauté for 2 to 3 minutes. Add the salt and pepper and continue to sauté for 2 minutes. Add the egg and whisk until well combined (about 30 seconds). Finally, add the parmesan cheese, mix well, and remove from heat. Spread the vegetable mixture on top of toasted baguette slices.

RISOTTO AL NERO DI SEPPIA
CUTTLEFISH ON BLACK RICE

Serves 1

4 ounces fresh, cleaned cuttlefish
1 tablespoon olive oil
1 teaspoon yellow onion, chopped
¼ cup dry white wine
⅓ cup arborio rice
2 cups fresh fish stock (see below)
⅛ teaspoon black squid ink (found in gourmet specialty stores or online)
3 leaves of Boston or butter lettuce
Diced vine-ripe tomato, for garnish

On a hot outdoor barbecue grill, stove-top griddle, or in a sauté pan over medium-high heat, grill the cuttlefish for several minutes until tender (about 5 to 8 minutes). Remove from heat and set aside.

In a small pot over medium-high heat, add the olive oil and onion and cook until onions are translucent. Add the white wine and rice and continue to cook until wine is reduced. Add the fish stock and cook for about 10 minutes, stirring often. Mix in the squid ink and continue to cook and stir until the liquid is absorbed.

Remove pan from heat. On a serving plate, arrange the lettuce leaves and place the cuttlefish on top. Place the black rice mixture on top of the cuttlefish and garnish with the diced tomato.

Chef's note: Cuttlefish are marine animals, similar to squid, with large eyes, eight arms, and two tentacles to secure their prey. They are caught for food in the Mediterranean and are popular in Italy.

FRESH FISH STOCK

2 tablespoons extra virgin olive oil
½ medium yellow onion, chopped
1 gallon water
2 stalks celery, chopped
1 medium carrot, peeled and chopped
1 teaspoon salt
1 teaspoon black pepper
1 teaspoon fresh thyme
2 to 3 cups of fish bones, or crab, lobster, or shrimp shells.

In a stock pot over medium-high heat, heat the olive oil and cook the onion until translucent. Add the water, celery, carrot, salt, pepper, thyme, and fish bones and seafood shells. Allow to boil about 10 minutes, then reduce heat to low. Simmer for about 45 minutes. Remove from heat and strain. Extra stock can be stored in the freezer.

INSALATA AI FRUTTI DI MARE
MIXED SEAFOOD SALAD
Serves 1

3 live Manila clams
3 live New Zealand green mussels
4 fresh, cleaned baby calamari, tubes and tentacles
6 fresh shrimp, shelled and deveined
1 tablespoon vine-ripe tomato, finely diced
2 pinches fresh Italian parsley, finely chopped
2 tablespoons lemon dressing (see page 24)
2 cups mixed baby greens
3 Belgian endive leaves

Into a boiling pot of lightly salted water, add all the seafood and cook about 5 minutes, or until the clams and mussels open. Remove and drain seafood, and set aside.

Next, in a sauté pan, add the lemon dressing, tomato, and parsley. Add the seafood to the pan and toss well to coat.

On a serving plate, arrange the mixed baby greens in the center and add the mussels around the greens. Place the Belgian endive leaves between the shells, and top the greens with the remaining seafood, tomato, parsley, and pan juices, including the lemon dressing.

Two thousand years ago in the Mediterranean region, Italian cooks were baking flour dough on a large stone heated in the fire, achieving a crisp but fluffy flatbread. Eventually, wood-fired ovens replaced the open fires and hot stones. Using such ovens, the Neapolitans created what many pizza aficionados to this day consider the quintessential pizza: a soft thin crust, lightly charred from wood-oven baking and infused with smoky flavor, brushed sparingly with a long-simmered tomato sauce made from the ripest of Italian tomatoes, topped with a sprinkling of fresh mozzarella cheese, and finished − immediately after the pie is pulled from the oven − with a few freshly torn basil leaves and a drizzle of extra virgin olive oil. Just as a pasta dish is, to an Italian, more about the pasta than the sauce, Italian pizza is about the crust. The toppings are always savory and delicious, but they are also few and never overwhelming.

PIZZE

In keeping with the spirit and soul of these Italian traditions, *Toscana* delivers some of the most incredibly tasty pizza combinations while using the best Italian "OO" flour and baking them in the restaurant's glowing wood-fired oven. Chef Hugo offers the traditional *Margherita* pizza − tomato, basil and cheese − with the perfect blistered crust and moist center, as well as other mouthwatering pies such as *Napoli*, *Caterina*, and *Susanna*.

For those who have yet to add a wood-fired oven to their kitchen or backyard, rest assured that all the pizzas in this chapter can be made in a conventional oven (best if cooked on a pizza stone) and even on the grill. However, Chef Hugo urges you to at least start dreaming of a wood-fired oven of your own.

I REMEMBER THE ORIGINAL EXECUTIVE CHEF WAS VERY OPPOSED TO INCLUDING PIZZA ON *TOSCANA'S* MENU. HE DIDN'T WANT THE *TRATTORIA* TO BE CONSIDERED A *PIZZERIA*. SO JUST PRIOR TO OPENING THE RESTAURANT WE NEGOTIATED A PIZZA-TASTING EVENING AT MIKE AND KATHIE'S HOME IN AN EFFORT TO CONVINCE HIM TO INCLUDE PIZZA ON THE MENU.

I THINK WE MADE 21 PIZZAS! HE WOULD TASTE A LITTLE, THEN DISCARD EACH PIZZA LIKE A KING WAVING OFF A BAD COURT JESTER. OCCASIONALLY HE MADE A MUMBLED COMMENT TO HIS SON IN ITALIAN AND WAITED FOR THE NEXT PIZZA VICTIM. AT THE END OF THE EVENING HE COUNTER-OFFERED: MAYBE ONE OF KATHIE'S AND ONE OF MIKE'S WOULD MAKE THE CUT TO THE MENU BUT THEY WOULD BE RELEGATED TO THE APPETIZER SECTION ONLY. THE REST OF THE MENU WAS HIS. WE ACCEPTED THE DEAL, BUT WE DECLARED WE WERE PERMANENTLY FINISHED EATING PIZZA—UNTIL THE FIRST ONE CAME OUT OF THE RESTAURANT'S NEW WOOD-BURNING OVEN.

JOEL SILL
Friend, Investor and Board Member

IMPASTO PER PIZZE

FRESH PIZZA DOUGH

Makes 8 (10-inch) pizzas

2 cups warm water	*1¼ teaspoon sugar*
1¼ teaspoon dry yeast	*2 tablespoons extra virgin olive oil*
1 teaspoon salt	*6 cups Italian "OO" Flour*

In a mixing bowl, add the warm water, yeast, salt, sugar, and olive oil, and whisk until the yeast is dissolved and activated (about 2 minutes). Pour the mixture into a mixer using the dough hook, and set to slow speed. Add the flour. When all the flour is added, speed up the machine for 1 minute until a dough ball is formed. Remove the dough and place on a floured countertop and allow to rest about 5 minutes. Divide the dough into 8 "balls," cover with damp cloth, and let rise for 15 minutes. The dough is now ready to use.

Chef's note: "OO" flour is the choice of pizza bakers in Italy. The "OO" signifies the flour has been finely ground, achieving a super-soft consistency and supple texture, which makes a crispier crust. This high-quality flour can be found in specialty markets or ordered online.

PIZZA MARGHERITA
FRESH BASIL & TOMATO

Makes 1 (10- to 12-inch) pizza

1 (7 ounce) ball fresh pizza dough (see page 89)
¾ cup fresh tomato sauce (see page 103)
3 ounces shredded mozzarella cheese
¼ teaspoon dried oregano
Fresh basil leaves

Dust a smooth working surface with flour. Place one pizza dough ball in the center. Flatten the dough into a disc shape with fingers. Next, roll the dough with a rolling pin until the dough is thin and reaches a diameter of 10 to 12 inches. Spoon the tomato sauce evenly over the top and sprinkle generously with the mozzarella cheese.

Using a metal or wood peel, place the pizza in a wood-fired oven, away from the fire, and let bake for several minutes. Turn the pizza 180 degrees and continue baking for another few minutes or until crust is golden brown and the cheese is bubbly. Remove pizza from the oven. Add a pinch of dried oregano and arrange the fresh basil leaves on top.

Chef's note: If using a conventional oven, preheat the oven and a pizza stone set on the middle rack for 30 minutes at 500 degrees F. When heated, place the pizza directly on the stone. Bake for approximately 6 minutes.

PIZZA ALLA CATERINA
GORGONZOLA, RADICCHIO & TOASTED WALNUTS
Makes 1 (10- to 12-inch) pizza

Toscana co-founder Kathie Gordon learned this recipe at home before passing it on to the restaurant. Although toasted walnuts are optional, she insists it is the walnuts that make the pizza.

1 (7 ounce) ball fresh pizza dough (see page 89)
3 ounces shredded mozzarella cheese
1 tablespoon gorgonzola, crumbled
¼ cup fresh radicchio, cut into julienne strips
1 tablespoon chopped toasted walnuts (optional)
Extra virgin olive oil, as needed

Dust a smooth working surface with flour. Place one pizza dough ball in the center. Flatten the dough into a disc shape with fingers. Next, roll the dough with a rolling pin until the dough is thin and reaches a diameter of 10 to 12 inches. Sprinkle generously with the mozzarella cheese. Arrange the crumbled gorgonzola and *radicchio* on top.

Using a metal or wood peel, place the pizza in a wood-fired oven, away from the fire, and let bake for several minutes. Turn the pizza 180 degrees and continue baking for another few minutes or until crust is golden brown and the cheese is bubbly. Remove pizza from the oven and arrange the toasted walnuts on top (if desired). Finish with a drizzle of extra virgin olive oil.

If using a conventional oven, preheat the oven with a pizza stone set on the middle rack for 30 minutes at 500 degrees F. When heated, place the pizza directly on the stone. Bake for approximately 6 minutes.

PIZZA AL PROSCIUTTO

FRESH TOMATO, MOZZARELLA, & PROSCIUTTO CRUDO

Makes 1 (10- to 12-inch) pizza

1 (7 ounce) ball fresh pizza dough (see page 89)
¾ cup fresh tomato sauce (see page 103)
3 ounces shredded mozzarella cheese
2 ounces prosciutto crudo, thinly sliced

Dust a smooth working surface with flour. Place one pizza dough ball in the center. Flatten the dough into a disc shape with fingers. Next, roll the dough with a rolling pin until the dough is thin and reaches a diameter of 10 to 12 inches. Spoon the tomato sauce evenly over the top and sprinkle generously with the mozzarella cheese.

Using a metal or wood peel, place the pizza in a wood-fired oven, away from the fire, and let bake for several minutes. Turn the pizza 180 degrees and continue baking for another few minutes or until crust is golden brown and the cheese is bubbly. Remove pizza from the oven and arrange the slices of prosciutto on top.

If using a conventional oven, preheat the oven with a pizza stone set on the middle rack for 30 minutes at 500 degrees F. When heated, place the pizza directly on the stone, and cook for approximately 6 minutes.

OUR KIDS HAVE GROWN UP HERE. WE'VE HAD COUNTLESS MEALS AT THE FAMILY TABLE AND CELEBRATIONS IN THE WINE ROOM. IT'S ONE OF THE ONLY THINGS IN BRENTWOOD THAT'S AGED WELL WITHOUT PLASTIC SURGERY. *MILLE GRAZIE!*

SUSAN HARRIS & PAUL WITT

PIZZA ALLE QUATTRO STAGIONI
ANCHOVY, ARTICHOKE, CAPERS, KALAMATA OLIVES, & PROSCIUTTO COTTO

Makes 1 (10- to 12-inch) pizza

1 (7 ounce) ball fresh pizza dough (see page 89)
¾ cup fresh tomato sauce (see page 103)
3 ounces shredded mozzarella cheese
4 or 5 slices hand-packed Italian anchovy filets
4 marinated baby artichokes, sliced
Kalamata olives, pitted and chopped, as desired
1 teaspoon capers
2 ounces prosciutto cotto, thinly sliced

Dust a smooth working surface with flour. Place one pizza dough ball in the center. Flatten the dough into a disc shape with fingers. Next, roll the dough with a rolling pin until the dough is thin and reaches a diameter of 10 to 12 inches. Spoon the tomato sauce evenly over the top and sprinkle generously with the mozzarella cheese. Arrange the anchovy, artichoke slices, kalamata olives, and capers on top.

Using a metal or wood peel, place the pizza in a wood-fired oven, away from the fire, and let bake for several minutes. Turn the pizza 180 degrees and continue baking for another few minutes or until crust is golden brown and the cheese is bubbly. Remove pizza from the oven and arrange the slices of prosciutto cotto on top.

If using a conventional oven, preheat the oven with a pizza stone set on the middle rack for 30 minutes at 500 degrees F. When heated, place the pizza directly on the stone, and cook for approximately 6 minutes.

Chef's note: Prosciutto cotto is Italian prosciutto that has been pre-cooked, as opposed to prosciutto crudo which is raw (although because of its curing, is ready to eat). Also, we use marinated artichoke hearts in the jar, found at most markets.

PIZZA ALLA SUSANNA
MOZZARELLA & ARUGULA

Makes 1 (10- to 12-inch) pizza

"We learned this pizza recipe from Susan Harris, famed television writer-producer and an original investor in Toscana. She had just returned from her first visit to Italy, and insisted we had to add this to the menu. She was right!"

Mike & Kathie Gordon

1 (7 ounce) ball fresh pizza dough (see page 89)
3 ounces shredded mozzarella cheese
4 ounces fresh arugula
Extra virgin olive oil

Dust a smooth working surface with flour. Place one pizza dough ball in the center. Flatten the dough into a disc shape with fingers. Next, roll the dough with a rolling pin until the dough is thin and reaches a diameter of 10 to 12 inches. Sprinkle generously with the mozzarella cheese.

Using a metal or wood peel, place the pizza in a wood-fired oven, away from the fire, and let bake for several minutes. Turn the pizza 180 degrees and continue baking for another few minutes or until crust is golden brown and the cheese is bubbly. Remove pizza from the oven and arrange the arugula on top. Drizzle a little extra virgin olive oil and serve.

If using a conventional oven, preheat the oven with a pizza stone set on the middle rack for 30 minutes at 500 degrees F. When heated, place the pizza directly on the stone, and cook for approximately 6 minutes.

PIZZA SUSANNA HAS MADE THE GENERATIONAL LEAP THAT BINDS THE CLIMAN FAMILY IN OUR LOVE AND AFFECTION FOR TOSCANA.

LORI & SANDY CLIMAN

PIZZA ALLA NAPOLI

ANCHOVY, CAPERS, & KALAMATA OLIVES

Makes 1 (10- to 12-inch) pizza

1 (7 ounce) ball fresh pizza dough (see page 89)
¾ cup fresh tomato sauce (see page 103)
3 ounces shredded mozzarella cheese
4 or 5 hand-packed Italian anchovy filets
Kalamata olives, pitted and halved, as desired
1 teaspoon capers

Dust a smooth working surface with flour. Place one pizza dough ball in the center. Flatten the dough into a disc shape with fingers. Next, roll the dough with a rolling pin until the dough is thin and reaches a diameter of 10 to 12 inches. Spoon the tomato sauce evenly over the top and sprinkle generously with the mozzarella cheese. Arrange the anchovy filets, olives, and capers on top.

Using a metal or wood peel, place the pizza in a wood-fired oven, away from the fire, and let bake for several minutes. Turn the pizza 180 degrees and continue baking for another few minutes or until crust is golden brown and the cheese is bubbly. Remove pizza from the oven and serve.

If using a conventional oven, preheat the oven with a pizza stone set on the middle rack for 30 minutes at 500 degrees F. When heated place the pizza directly on the stone. Bake for approximately 6 minutes.

FOR MYSELF AND MY FAMILY *TOSCANA* IS A PLACE TO RELAX, ENJOY SPECTACULAR FOOD, AND FEEL LIKE WE ARE "OWNERS." IT IS A ONE OF A KIND RESTAURANT. HAPPY 20TH FROM ALL OF US TO ALL OF YOU.

HOWARD WEITZMAN

FOCACCINA

FRESH ROSEMARY AND EXTRA VIRGIN OLIVE OIL

Makes 1 (10- to 12-inch) pizza

1 (7 ounce) ball fresh pizza dough (see page 89)
¼ teaspoon fresh chopped rosemary
Extra virgin olive oil, as needed

Dust a smooth working surface with flour. Place one pizza dough ball in the center. Flatten the dough into a disc shape with fingers. Next, roll the dough with a rolling pin until the dough is thin and reaches a diameter of 10 to 12 inches. With a fork or knife, poke holes into the dough so the dough will not rise when baked.

Using a metal or wood peel, place the pizza in a wood-fired oven, away from the fire, and let bake for several minutes. Turn the pizza 180 degrees and continue baking for another few minutes or until crust is golden brown. Remove focaccina from the oven and sprinkle the chopped rosemary on top. Finish with a liberal drizzle of extra virgin olive oil.

If using a conventional oven, preheat the oven with a pizza stone set on the middle rack for 30 minutes at 500 degrees F. When heated, place the pizza directly on the stone, and cook for approximately 6 minutes.

Pasta is synonymous with Italy, so what better way to honor the celebrated food than showcasing a selection of delectable recipes. *Toscana* serves many traditional pasta dishes along with exciting *risotti*, including some secret off-the-menu favorites. Without question, *Toscana* is best known for its freshness and quality of ingredients, and every pasta and *risotto* dish prepared at the trattoria is handcrafted with excellence in mind. The ever popular *tagliatelle alla bolognese* is loaded with prime ground beef and the sauce is always consistent, having been prepared in the same fashion since *Toscana* opened its doors twenty years ago. This incredible dish, as with all the pasta dishes served at *Toscana*, is never smothered in sauce—just enough to marry the tender noodles with the wonderful flavor of the sauce.

PASTE E
RISOTTI

Ask Kathie Gordon and she'll tell you *Toscana's paste* and *risotti* are made from the heart. "Our chefs and kitchen staff put their heart and soul into every dish they prepare." Kathie's personal favorite is the regularly requested *rigatoni alla contadina*. "I appreciate the wonderful texture, the rich tomato, and the crumbled bits of pancetta." Other *Toscana* hits include *capellini all' ortolana, spaghetti alle vongole*, the unusual *spaghetti alla bottarga, gnocchi al pesto, risotto al rosmarino*, and *ravioli di zucca*. And although these are all light, flavorful dishes, their beauty lies in their simplicity to make, especially after a long day at the office. "And feel free to experiment with something you haven't tried before," quips Francesco Greco. "Many of our guests order the same dish they've ordered for years because they enjoy a particular pasta and stand behind the old adage 'if it's not broke, don't fix it.' But when we introduce them to a new pasta or *risotto*, their response is always the same, 'I can't believe I haven't tried this before. Look what I've been missing!'"

SALSA DI POMODORO
TOSCANA'S HOMEMADE TOMATO SAUCE
Makes approximately 4 servings

1 tablespoon extra virgin olive oil
4 cups canned Italian tomatoes with juice (San Marzano)
1 cup water
4 fresh basil leaves
½ teaspoon salt

Heat the olive oil in a medium-size pot over medium heat. Blend the tomatoes and juice in a blender or Cuisinart until pureed. Add the water to the pot with the basil leaves and salt. Reduce heat and simmer for about 15 minutes.

SPAGHETTI AL POMODORO
SPAGHETTI WITH TOMATO AND BASIL

Serves 4

1 pound spaghetti
6 quarts water
½ tablespoon salt
3 cups fresh tomato sauce (see page 103)
2 fresh basil leaves, whole
2 tablespoons butter
5 tablespoons fresh grated parmesan cheese

Prepare the pasta by boiling 6 quarts of water with the salt. Add the pasta and stir, returning to a rapid boil. Cook uncovered according to package directions until al dente, stirring occasionally.

While pasta is cooking, in a large sauté pan over medium-high heat, add the tomato sauce, basil, and butter. Cook until butter is melted. Remove the pasta from the heat, drain, and add to the sauce. Toss well. Add the parmesan cheese and toss again allowing cheese to melt. Transfer to individual serving plates and serve immediately.

I DIDN'T REALIZE THE RESTAURANT WAS CLOSED WHEN I PULLED ON THE DOOR. MUCH TO MY SURPRISE, I SAW A FAMILIAR FACE: IT WAS ALBERTO! HE QUIETLY UNLOCKED THE DOOR AND SCOOTED US INSIDE SAYING TO HIS COLLEAGUES, "THESE ARE OLD FRIENDS." WE HAD PERFECTLY PREPARED *PENNE ARRABIATA* AND SPAGHETTI *POMODORO* AND GREAT WINE. FROM THAT DAY FORWARD, *TOSCANA* BECAME OUR "LOCAL" AND OUR FAVORITE RESTAURANT.

MARK KANER

CAPELLINI ALL' ORTOLANA
ANGEL HAIR PASTA WITH FRESH VEGETABLES AND TOMATO SAUCE
Serves 4

Toscana's style of preparing pasta is very simple. Cook the pasta and sauce separately, add the cooked pasta to the sauce, and toss well before serving.

1 pound angel hair or capellini pasta
6 quarts water
½ tablespoon salt
1 tablespoon extra virgin olive oil
4 cups fresh tomato sauce (see page 103)
2 cups small diced mixed vegetables (carrot, celery,
    peas, white mushroom, zucchini), in equal amounts
Pinch salt
Pinch black pepper
3 tablespoons butter
5 tablespoons fresh grated parmesan cheese

Prepare the pasta by boiling 6 quarts of water with the salt. Add the pasta and stir, returning to a rapid boil. Cook uncovered according to the package directions until al dente, stirring occasionally

While pasta is cooking, in a large sauté pan over medium-high heat, add the olive oil, mixed vegetables, salt, and pepper. Sauté for about 5 minutes. Add the tomato sauce and cook for another 5 minutes, then add the butter.

Remove the pasta from the heat, drain, and add to the sauce. Toss well. Add the parmesan cheese and toss again allowing cheese to melt. Serve immediately.

Chef's note: *Capellini* pasta are long strands of very thin pasta, similar to angel hair, but slightly thicker. Often *capellini* and angel hair are referred to as the same pasta.

PENNETTE ALLA CARRETTIERA
PENNE WITH ANCHOVY, CAPERS, GARLIC, OLIVES, AND TOMATO

Serves 4

1 pound penne pasta
6 quarts water
½ tablespoon salt
2 tablespoons extra virgin olive oil
2 garlic cloves, smashed
4 anchovy fillets, chopped
4 teaspoons capers
4 tablespoons black kalamata olives, pitted and sliced
3 cups fresh tomato sauce (see page 103)
Italian parsley, finely chopped for garnish

Prepare the pasta by boiling 6 quarts of water with the salt. Add the pasta and stir, returning to a rapid boil. Cook uncovered according to package directions until al dente, stirring occasionally.

While pasta is cooking, in a large sauté pan over medium-high heat, add the olive oil. When hot, add the garlic and cook until golden brown. Add the anchovy, capers, olives, and tomato sauce. Cook for several minutes and discard the garlic.

Remove the pasta from the heat, drain, and add to the sauce. Toss well. Transfer to individual serving plates and top with Italian parsley. Serve immediately.

Chef's note: Penne pasta is one of the more famous Italian pasta shapes: tube-shaped pasta with angled cuts on the end, resembling a quill or pen point.

SPAGHETTI CON CALAMARI E SALVIA
SPAGHETTI WITH CALAMARI AND SAGE

Serves 4

1 pound spaghetti
6 quarts water
½ tablespoon salt
2 tablespoons extra virgin olive oil
2 garlic cloves, smashed
6 fresh sage leaves
2 cups fresh, cleaned calamari, tubes and tentacles
½ cup dry white wine
3 teaspoons salt
2 teaspoons crushed red pepper flakes
1 teaspoon fresh Italian parsley, finely chopped

Prepare the pasta by boiling 6 quarts of water with the salt. Add the pasta and stir, returning to a rapid boil. Cook uncovered according to package directions until al dente, stirring occasionally.

While pasta is cooking, in a large sauté pan over medium-high heat, add the olive oil. When hot, add the garlic and cook until golden brown. Add the sage leaves, and cook for several minutes, careful not to burn the leaves. Add the calamari, white wine, salt, red pepper, and parsley. Cook until calamari is tender, about 4 to 5 minutes, being careful not to overcook it. Discard the garlic.

Remove the pasta from the heat, drain and add to the sauce. Toss well. Transfer to individual serving plates, and serve immediately with a drizzle of olive oil.

TOSCANA PROBABLY ADDS TO MY WAISTLINE BUT BEING THERE ADDS TO MY HEALTH AND WELL-BEING.

GERALIN CLARK

TRENETTE AL PESTO
LINGUINE WITH PESTO
Serves 4

1 pound linguine
6 quarts water
½ tablespoon salt
Fresh pesto (see below)

Prepare the pasta by boiling 6 quarts of water with the salt. Add the pasta and stir, returning to a rapid boil. Cook uncovered according to package directions until al dente, stirring occasionally. When done, remove from heat, drain and set aside.

Put the pesto in a large sauté pan and add the cooked pasta to the pan. Mix well. Transfer to individual serving plates. Serve immediately.

Chef's note: Like fettuccine, linguine is a flat pasta but narrow like spaghetti. The name means "little tongues" in Italian.

PESTO
Makes approximately 6 servings

1 cup fresh basil leaves, with stems removed
¼ cup fresh pine nuts
2 garlic cloves, peeled
½ cup fresh grated parmesan cheese
1 teaspoon salt
½ cup olive oil

In a blender, add the basil, pine nuts, garlic, parmesan cheese, salt, and olive oil. Blend until smooth. More or less olive oil can be added to desired consistency.

Chef's note: Often extra virgin olive oil can make pesto taste bitter so use only olive oil. It can also be noted that extra pesto sauce can be frozen up to one month.

I SEARCH THE WORLD SEEKING FINE PESTO. IT IS COMFORTING TO KNOW THAT THIS CRAVING OF MINE CAN ALWAYS BE SATISFIED TO THE HIGHEST QUALITY AT *TOSCANA*. CONGRATULATIONS!

DAN AYKROYD

RIGATONI ALLA CONTADINA
RIGATONI WITH PANCETTA, ONION, AND TOMATO

Serves 4

1 pound rigatoni pasta

6 quarts water

½ tablespoon salt

3 tablespoons olive oil

2 small yellow onions, sliced

9 ounces pancetta, thickly sliced and chopped into ¼ inch dice

¾ cup dry white wine

2 cups fresh tomato sauce (see page 103)

1½ cups water

2 bay leaves

2 tablespoons butter

5 tablespoons fresh grated parmesan cheese, plus extra for garnish

Heat the olive oil in a medium sauté pan over medium-high heat. Add the onions and cook until translucent, about 10 minutes. Remove from heat and set aside.

In a separate large sauté pan over medium-high heat, add the pancetta and cook until almost crispy. Add the cooked onions and white wine and simmer until wine is reduced. Add the tomato sauce and water and continue to simmer, about 20 minutes. Add the bay leaves and simmer an additional 10 minutes.

While sauce is simmering, prepare the pasta by boiling 6 quarts of water with the salt. Add the pasta and stir, returning to a rapid boil. Cook uncovered, according to package directions until al dente, stirring occasionally. When done, remove from heat and drain.

Remove the bay leaves from the sauce and add the cooked pasta, butter, and parmesan cheese. Mix well until cheese has melted and transfer to individual serving plates. Sprinkle extra parmesan cheese on top and serve immediately.

Chef's note: Rigatoni is a tube-shaped pasta, but larger than penne. Rigatoni is usually ridged to help hold sauce, and the ends are not cut at an angle like penne.

TAGLIATELLE ALLA BOLOGNESE
FETTUCCINE WITH BEEF RAGU

Serves 4

¼ cup olive oil
16 ounces ground chuck beef
1 tablespoon garlic, peeled and minced
2 tablespoons fresh chopped rosemary
½ teaspoon ground nutmeg
1 teaspoon salt
½ teaspoon pepper
1 carrot, diced
1 small bunch celery (about 6 short stalks), diced
1 medium-size yellow onion, diced
1½ cups red wine
3 cups fresh tomato sauce (see page 103)
4 cups chicken stock
1 pound tagliatelle pasta
6 quarts water
½ tablespoon salt
2 tablespoons butter
5 tablespoons fresh grated parmesan cheese

In a stock pot over medium-high heat, add the olive oil. When hot, add the ground beef, garlic, rosemary, nutmeg, salt, and pepper, and cook until beef is brown and crumbled (about 25 minutes). Add the chopped carrot, celery and onion, and cook for another 15 minutes. Add the red wine, lower the heat to simmer, and cook until wine is reduced. Add the tomato sauce and chicken stock and let simmer on very low heat for about 1½ hours.

Prepare the pasta by boiling 6 quarts of water with the salt. Add the pasta and stir, returning to a rapid boil. Cook uncovered according to package directions until al dente, stirring occasionally. When done, remove from heat, drain and add the pasta, butter and parmesan cheese to the bolognese. Mix well until cheese has melted and transfer to individual serving plates. Serve immediately.

Chef's note: This wonderful fettuccine dish can also be prepared with *Toscana's* homemade Veal Ragu (see next recipe).

RAGU DI VITELLO

VEAL RAGU

Serves 4

3 tablespoons extra virgin olive oil

2 garlic cloves, finely chopped

½ large yellow onion, finely chopped

1 carrot, finely chopped

4 stalks celery, finely chopped

16 ounces fresh ground veal

1 teaspoon salt

¼ teaspoon black pepper

½ cup dry white wine

1 cup chicken stock

¼ teaspoon fresh chopped rosemary

1 small sage leaf, chopped

1 pound tagliatelle pasta

6 quarts water

½ tablespoon salt

2 tablespoons butter

5 tablespoons fresh grated parmesan cheese

In a large sauce pan or small stock pot over medium-high heat, add the olive oil. When hot, add the onion and garlic and saute until onions are translucent.

In a blender or Cuisinart, finely mince the carrot and celery, and add to pan. Cook for 5 minutes. Add the ground veal and stir, cooking another 2 minutes. Add the salt and pepper and stir, cooking for an additional 2 minutes. Add the white wine and let reduce about 10 minutes. Add the chicken stock, rosemary, and sage, and reduce liquid by about half.

Next, prepare the pasta by boiling 6 quarts of water with the salt. Add the pasta and stir, returning to a rapid boil. Cook uncovered according to package directions until al dente, stirring occasionally. When done, remove from heat, drain and add the pasta, butter, and parmesan cheese to the veal ragu. Mix well until cheese is melted and transfer to individual serving plates. Serve immediately.

MARK + ALBERTO + ANTONIO = *TOSCANA*. YOU GUYS ARE THE HEART AND SOUL OF OUR FAVORITE RESTAURANT.

JAY AND ANNE SURES FAMILY

TAGLIATELLE CON PORCINI
FETTUCCINE WITH PORCINI MUSHROOMS

Serves 4

3 tablespoons olive oil
1 clove garlic, smashed
12 ounces sliced fresh porcini mushrooms
1 teaspoon salt
1 teaspoon black pepper
Splash white wine (about 1 tablespoon)
1 pound tagliatelle pasta
6 quarts water
½ tablespoon salt
1 teaspoon fresh Italian parsley, finely chopped
2 tablespoons butter (optional)

Heat the olive oil in a medium sauté pan over medium-high heat. Add the garlic and cook until garlic is soft and lightly brown. Add the chopped porcini mushrooms, salt, pepper, and white wine. Allow to simmer until wine is reduced, about 5 minutes.

While mushroom sauce is simmering, prepare the pasta by boiling 6 quarts of water with the salt. Add the pasta and stir, returning to a rapid boil. Cook uncovered according to package directions until al dente, stirring occasionally. When done, remove from heat and drain.

Add the cooked pasta to the mushroom pan and toss well. Add the parsley and butter, if desired. Discard the garlic and transfer to individual serving plates. Serve immediately.

Chef's note: Fettuccine, meaning "little ribbons" in Italian, are flat, thick noodles, which are wider than linguine. The flavor will not be compromised if you choose to use portobello mushrooms in place of porcini.

SPAGHETTI ALLE VONGOLE

SPAGHETTI WITH CLAMS

Serves 4

1 pound spaghetti
6 quarts water
½ tablespoon salt
4 tablespoons extra virgin olive oil
2 pounds live baby Manila clams
2 garlic cloves, smashed
½ cup dry white wine
¾ cup fish stock (see page 79)
½ teaspoon salt
¼ teaspoon crushed red pepper flakes

Prepare the pasta by boiling 6 quarts of water with the salt. Add the pasta and stir, returning to a rapid boil. Cook uncovered according to package directions until al dente, stirring occasionally.

While pasta is cooking, in a large sauté pan over medium-high heat, add the olive oil. When hot, add the garlic and cook until golden brown. Add the clams, white wine, fish stock, salt, and crushed red pepper. Reduce heat and let cook until clams open (about 5 minutes). Discard the garlic. Remove the pasta from the heat, drain and add to the sauce. Toss well. Transfer to individual serving plates and serve immediately.

I CRAVE THE SHRIMP *INSALATA* BUT NOBODY MAKES BETTER LINGUINE & CLAMS. WE HAD OUR SALTAIR AVE. "POTLUCK" DINNER IN THE PRIVATE WINE ROOM. NOW THAT IS A POTLUCK DINNER!

BRUCE MELLON

SPAGHETTI AI RICCI DI MARE

SPAGHETTI WITH SEA URCHIN (UNI)

Serves 4

1 pound spaghetti
6 quarts water
½ tablespoon salt
1 tablespoon extra virgin olive oil
2 garlic cloves, smashed
12 pieces sushi-grade uni (reserve 4 uncooked pieces for garnish)
½ cup dry white wine
½ tablespoon fresh Italian parsley, finely chopped
½ teaspoon crushed red pepper flakes

Prepare the pasta by boiling 6 quarts of water with the salt. Add the pasta and stir, returning to a rapid boil. Cook uncovered according to package directions until al dente, stirring occasionally. When done, remove from heat and drain.

While pasta is cooking, heat the olive oil in a large sauté pan over medium-high heat. Add the garlic and cook until golden brown. Add 8 pieces of uni, white wine, Italian parsley, and crushed red pepper. Lower heat and let cook until wine is reduced, about 5 minutes.

Discard the garlic, add the cooked pasta to the pan and mix well. Transfer to individual serving plates and place 1 piece of uncooked uni on top of each pasta. Finish by pouring over the remaining pan juices. Serve immediately.

SPAGHETTI AI FRUTTI DI MARE

SPAGHETTI WITH SEAFOOD

Serves 4

2 tablespoons olive oil

2 cloves garlic, smashed

9 ounces shrimp, cleaned and deveined

10 ounces live baby Manila clams

8 ounces live New Zealand green mussels

11 ounces fresh, cleaned
     calamari, tubes and tentacles

½ cup white wine

3 cups fresh tomato sauce (see page 103)

½ cup fresh fish stock (see page 79)

1 pound spaghetti

6 quarts water

4 prawns, whole

1 tablespoon fresh Italian parsley,
     finely chopped, for garnish

Drizzle of extra virgin olive oil

Heat the olive oil in a large sauté pan over medium-high heat. Add the garlic and cook until golden brown. Add the shrimp, clams, mussels, and calamari and cook until clams and mussels open. When shrimp and *calamari* are tender, remove from pan and set aside. Add the white wine, tomato sauce, and fish stock to the pan and continue to cook until the wine is reduced about 5 minutes. While wine is reducing, grill or sauté the prawns on high heat until tender and set aside.

Meanwhile, prepare the pasta by boiling 6 quarts of water with the salt. Add the pasta and stir, returning to a rapid boil. Cook uncovered according to package directions until al dente, stirring occasionally. When done, remove from heat and drain.

Next, discard the garlic from the pan and return the shrimp and *calamari* to the sauce. Add the cooked pasta to the pan and mix well. Transfer to individual serving plates and top each serving with a grilled prawn, the Italian parsley, and a drizzle of extra virgin olive oil. Serve immediately.

KATHIE, MIKE, FRANCESCO, ANTONIO, MARK, ALBERTO, ET AL., FOR ALL THE HUGS, FOOD, AND MEMORIES. HERE'S TO 20 MORE, AND THEN SOME.

JOE & RITA COHEN

SPAGHETTI ALLA BOTTARGA
SPAGHETTI WITH SHAVED RED MULLET ROE

Serves 4

1 pound spaghetti
6 quarts water
½ tablespoon salt
1 tablespoon extra virgin olive oil
2 garlic cloves, smashed
½ cup dry white wine
½ tablespoon fresh Italian parsley, finely chopped
½ teaspoon crushed red pepper flakes
Dried red mullet roe (bottarga), as desired

Prepare the pasta by boiling 6 quarts of water with the salt. Add the pasta and stir, returning to a rapid boil. Cook uncovered according to package directions until al dente, stirring occasionally. When done, remove from heat, drain and set aside.

Meanwhile, heat the olive oil in a large sauté pan over medium-high heat. Add the garlic and cook until golden brown. Add the white wine, Italian parsley, and crushed red pepper. Lower heat and let cook until wine is reduced, about 5 minutes.

Discard the garlic, add the cooked pasta to the pan and mix well. Transfer to individual serving plates and grate the *bottarga* over each pasta as if grating cheese. Finish by pouring the remaining pan juices over the pasta. Serve immediately.

Chef's note: Once the taste of *bottarga* is developed, it is a welcomed addition to any of *Toscana's* non–tomato based seafood pastas.

SPAGHETTI ALL' ARAGOSTA
SPAGHETTI WITH LOBSTER

Serves 4

1 pound live Maine lobster
6 quarts water, for boiling lobster
1 pound spaghetti
6 quarts water, for boiling pasta
½ tablespoon salt
2 tablespoons olive oil
2 cloves garlic, smashed
½ cup white wine
3 cups fresh tomato sauce (see page 103)
½ cup fresh fish stock (see page 79)
1 tablespoon fresh Italian parsley, finely chopped, for garnish
Drizzle of extra virgin olive oil

In a large pot boil water and add the lobster and cook for 10 minutes. Begin timing once the water returns to a boil. Remove lobster and let cool until easy to handle. Remove tail meat and roughly chop. Carefully remove claw meat and keep intact for garnish.

Prepare the pasta by boiling 6 quarts of water with the salt. Add the pasta and stir, returning to a rapid boil. Cook uncovered according to package directions until al dente, stirring occasionally. When done, remove from heat and drain.

Heat the olive oil in a large sauté pan over medium-high heat. Add the garlic and cook until golden brown. Add the white wine, tomato sauce, and fish stock and continue to cook until the wine is reduced, about 5 minutes. Discard the garlic, add the cooked pasta and the lobster tail meat to the pan, and mix well. Transfer to individual serving plates and top with the reserved claw meat. Finish with Italian parsley and a drizzle of extra virgin olive oil. Serve immediately.

SPAGHETTI CON LE TRIGLIE
SPAGHETTI WITH RED MULLET

Serves 4

1 pound spaghetti
6 quarts water
½ tablespoon salt
1 tablespoon extra virgin olive oil
2 garlic cloves, smashed
1 pound fresh red mullet filets, cut into 2-inch pieces
1 teaspoon salt
½ teaspoon crushed red pepper flakes
½ cup dry white wine
½ teaspoon fresh Italian parsley, finely chopped

Prepare the pasta by boiling 6 quarts of water with the salt. Add the pasta and stir, returning to a rapid boil. Cook uncovered, according to package directions until al dente, stirring occasionally. Remove from heat and drain.

While pasta is cooking, heat the olive oil in a large sauté pan over medium-high heat. Add the garlic and cook until golden brown. Add the red mullet filets, salt, crushed red pepper, white wine, and Italian parsley. Lower heat and let cook until wine is reduced and fish is moist and flakey, about 5 minutes.

Remove the fish and discard the garlic. Add the cooked pasta to the pan and mix well. Transfer to individual serving plates and arrange the fish on top. Finish by pouring over the remaining pan juices. Serve immediately.

Although all your dishes are tasty, we have our favorites: Peter loves the veal parmesan (burnt); Ginger eats the seafood pasta; Alex, the orecchiette with brisket; and Sam, penne with shrimp. Your food makes us smile.

THE BORT FAMILY

CONGRATS! TO KATHIE & MIKE, FRANCESCO AND THE ENTIRE STAFF ON A VERY SUCCESSFUL 20 YEARS!!! DAN & LUANA ROMANELLI

THERE IS NOWHERE ELSE WE WOULD RATHER BE FOR DINNER. SKIP & SHERRY MILLER FAMILY

The Toscana family makes certain that my family and I feel like royalty each and every time we visit. TOM ORTENBERG

WELL, IT'S ALMOST UNIMAGINABLE TO THINK ABOUT RESTAURANT LIFE IN L.A. WITHOUT TOSCANA—AND ITS SEAFOOD PASTA DISHES. CONGRATULATIONS TO FRANCESCO AND HIS BAND OF MERRY WAITERS WHO ALL COMBINE TO MAKE TOSCANA A JOY. ADAM LINTER

The food is always terrific and Antonella, the chefs, the waiters all make the experience of dining at Toscana an extraordinary occurrence. *John McClune*

THANKS FOR THE MOST CONSISTENTLY EXCELLENT ITALIAN CUISINE IN LOS ANGELES, AND FOR YOUR WARM HOSPITALITY! ROGER L. WERNER

TOSCANA IS PART OF THE FAMILY. WE GO, WE EAT, LAUGH, TELL STORIES AND HAVE A WONDERFUL TIME AND MEAL. GIL CATES

"THE MINESTRONE ON WINTER NIGHTS, THE SIMPLE QUALITY OF TOSCANA'S CUISINE, THE INCANDESCENT WARMTH OF THE PEOPLE—OUR PALS ALBERTO AND FRANCESCO—THE DISCRETE, UNPRETENTIOUS DECOR: ALL THESE QUALITIES ARE WHAT MAKES TOSCANA SO SPECIAL TO US AND OUR FAMILY, AND IT'S BEEN THAT WAY FOR 20 YEARS."

THE MICHAEL MANN FAMILY

Your food is always terrific, but it is the warmth of the staff and the feeling that you treat us as part of your family that keeps us coming back.

JAMIE & SCOTT HONOUR

WHAT IS THERE TO SAY ABOUT YOUR FOOD? SCRUMPTIOUS. MY FAVORITE, THE CHICKEN MILANESE, I DREAM ABOUT IT!!

ALANA & ELLIOT MEGDAL

I've searched the earth, including Italy for a restaurant with as consistently good food as Toscana and have come up empty.

RICHARD OFFSTEIN, M.D.

LOVE YOU ALL SO MUCH! ROBB AND I THANK YOU FOR THE MANY YEARS OF GREAT FOOD AND YOUR GENUINE FRIENDSHIPS!! XOXO. KAREN BELL & ROBB COX

TOSCANA IS MY FAVORITE PLACE TO TAKE MY FAMILY AND FRIENDS. I HAVE NEVER BEEN SO WARMLY GREETED, WELCOMED OR FED SO WELL. CONSISTENTLY!

JARL MOHN

TAGLIATELLE CON CARNE DI GRANCHIO

FETTUCCINE WITH KING CRAB

Serves 4

1 pound tagliatelle pasta
6 quarts water
½ tablespoon salt
2 tablespoons olive oil
2 cloves garlic, smashed
1 pound king crab meat, roughly chopped (reserve 4 large leg pieces for garnish)
½ cup white wine
½ cup fresh fish stock (see page 79)
1 tablespoon fresh Italian parsley, finely chopped, for garnish
Drizzle of extra virgin olive oil

Prepare the pasta by boiling 6 quarts of water with the salt. Add the pasta and stir, returning to a rapid boil. Cook uncovered according to package directions until al dente, stirring occasionally. When done, remove from heat and drain.

Meanwhile, heat the olive oil in a large sauté pan over medium-high heat. Add the garlic and cook until golden brown. Add the white wine and fish stock and continue to cook until the wine is reduced, about 5 minutes. Discard the garlic, add the cooked pasta and the king crab meat to the pan, and mix well. Transfer to individual serving plates and top with the reserved pieces of crab meat. Finish with Italian parsley and a drizzle of extra virgin olive oil. Serve immediately.

BUCATINI ALLA CARBONARA
BUCATINI WITH EGG AND PANCETTA

Serves 4

1 pound bucatini pasta
6 quarts water
½ tablespoon salt
1 cup pancetta, thinly sliced and diced small
4 egg yolks
3 tablespoons whipping cream
½ teaspoon cracked black pepper
2 tablespoons fresh grated pecorino cheese

Prepare the pasta by boiling 6 quarts of water with the salt. Add the pasta and stir, returning to a rapid boil. Cook uncovered according to package directions until al dente, stirring occasionally.

Meanwhile, add the pancetta to a large sauté pan over medium-high heat and cook until crispy. In a separate bowl, whisk the egg yolks, whipping cream, and black pepper until combined.

When pasta is cooked, remove from heat, drain, and add to the saucepan along with the egg and cream mixture. Toss in the cooked pancetta and pecorino cheese, and mix well. Transfer to individual serving plates and serve immediately.

Chef's note: Bucatini is a thick spaghetti-like pasta with a hole running through the center.

PAPPARDELLE AL CINGHIALE
PAPPARDELLE WITH WILD BOAR

Serves 4

12 ounces wild boar, cut into 1-inch cubes
2 carrots, chopped
3 celery stalks, chopped
2 cups red wine, divided
2 garlic cloves, smashed
2 fresh rosemary sprigs, 1 chopped
3 tablespoons extra virgin olive oil
1 garlic clove, chopped
2 cups fresh tomato sauce (see page 103)

2 cups chicken stock
1 teaspoon salt
¼ teaspoon black pepper
1 pound pappardelle pasta
6 quarts of water
½ tablespoon salt
2 ounces butter
¼ cup fresh grated parmesan cheese

In a large bowl add the wild boar, carrots, celery, 1 cup red wine, garlic, and 1 whole rosemary sprig. Mix well, and allow to marinate overnight in the refrigerator.

Drain the meat and transfer to a large (preheated) sauté pan over medium heat with the olive oil. Brown the meat on all sides. When brown, add the chopped garlic and chopped rosemary. Allow to cook for about 5 minutes. Add the remaining cup of red wine and allow to reduce, about 10 minutes. Add the tomato sauce, chicken stock, salt, and pepper. Lower heat to low, cover the pan, and let simmer over very low heat for 1½ hours, stirring occasionally.

Next, prepare the *pappardelle* by boiling 6 quarts of water with ½ tablespoon of salt. Add the pasta and stir, returning to a rapid boil. Cook uncovered according to package directions until al dente, stirring occasionally. When done, remove from heat and drain. Transfer pasta to the sauce pan and mix well. Add the butter and parmesan cheese and toss until incorporated. Transfer to individual serving plates and serve immediately.

Chef's note: Pappardelle is a wide, flat fettuccine pasta. The name derives from *"pappare,"* meaning to gobble up. Also note that wild boar may not be readily available; however, most butchers can order it for you.

MEZZE MANICHE ALLA NORMA
HALF RIGATONI WITH EGGPLANT
Serves 4

1 medium fresh eggplant
4 tablespoons olive oil
1 garlic clove, smashed
6 whole basil leaves
1 pound mezze maniche pasta
6 quarts water
½ tablespoon salt
1 ½ cups fresh tomato sauce (see page 103)
½ teaspoon salt
½ teaspoon black pepper
10 ounces dry ricotta salata, grated

Prepare the pasta by boiling 6 quarts of water with the salt. Add the pasta and stir, returning to a rapid boil. Cook uncovered according to package directions until al dente, stirring occasionally. Remove from heat and drain.

Meanwhile peel the eggplant and cut into 1-inch cubes. Next, heat the olive oil in a large sauté pan over medium-high heat, add the garlic and cook until golden brown. Add the eggplant along with the basil leaves and sauté for about 12 minutes.

Remove garlic. Add the tomato sauce, salt, and pepper to the pan with the eggplant and cook for another 5 minutes. Add the cooked pasta to the pan, mixing well. Transfer to individual serving plates and top with the ricotta salata. Serve immediately.

Chef's note: Mezze maniche is a pasta similar to penne but shorter and broader. You can also use rigatoni for this dish.

THE FOOD, THE PREPARATION, THE ATMOSPHERE MAKES *TOSCANA* THE QUINTESSENTIAL NEIGHBORHOOD RESTAURANT.

CHARLEY STEINER
Los Angeles Dodgers

ORECCHIETTE CON CIME DI RAPA E SALSICCE

LAMB'S EAR PASTA WITH RAPINI & SAUSAGE

Serves 4

1 pound fresh rapini
Water to cover rapini
½ tablespoon salt
2 tablespoons extra virgin olive oil
2 garlic cloves, smashed
1 pound Italian sausage, casing removed and crumbled
¼ teaspoon salt
¼ teaspoon crushed red pepper
9 ounces orecchiette pasta
5 quarts of water
½ tablespoon salt

In a pot of boiling salted water, add the rapini and cook for about 5 minutes. Remove *rapini*, drain, and press between paper towels to squeeze out any excess water. Coarsely chop *rapini* and set aside.

In a large sauté pan over medium-high heat, add the olive oil. When hot, add the garlic. Remove the sausage from the casing and add to pan with the salt and red pepper. Cook for about 4 to 5 minutes, or until the sausage is brown and crumbled.

Prepare the pasta by boiling 5 quarts of water with the salt. Add the pasta and stir, returning to a rapid boil. Cook uncovered according to package directions until al dente, stirring occasionally. Remove from heat and drain.

Add the cooked *rapini* to the pan and mix well. Discard the garlic and add the cooked pasta to the pan, tossing well. Transfer to individual serving plates and top with a drizzle of extra virgin olive oil. Serve immediately.

Chef's note: Orecchiette is a pasta that resembles a small ear, a dome-shaped pasta with a thin center and rough outer edge.

RIGATONI CON CARCIOFI
RIGATONI WITH ARTICHOKE
Serves 4

This is one of the original dishes at *Toscana*, but not found on the menu today.

Boiling salted water
16 fresh baby artichokes
3 tablespoons extra virgin olive oil
1 garlic clove, smashed
½ teaspoon white pepper
3 ounces fresh grated parmesan cheese, divided
⅓ cup of water or chicken stock
2 ounces butter
1 pound rigatoni
6 quarts of water
½ tablespoon salt

Boil a pot of salted water. While water is preparing to boil, remove all the outer leaves of the baby artichokes and thinly slice the chokes. Immediately add the sliced chokes to the boiling salted water and cook until tender, about 4 minutes. Remove chokes from heat, drain, and set aside.

In a large sauté pan over medium-high heat, add the olive oil. When hot, add the garlic and sauté until garlic is soft and golden brown. Add the cooked artichokes, along with salt and pepper and the water or stock. Reduce down and add the butter and 1 ounce of parmesan cheese.

Meanwhile, prepare the pasta by boiling 6 quarts of water with the salt. Add the pasta and stir, returning to a rapid boil. Cook uncovered according to package directions until al dente, stirring occasionally. Remove from heat and drain.

Discard the garlic from the pan and add the cooked pasta with another ounce of parmesan cheese. Toss well. Transfer to individual serving plates and top with the remaining ounce of parmesan cheese. Serve immediately.

GNOCCHI AL PESTO
GNOCCHI WITH PESTO

Serves 4

At Toscana, fresh-made gnocchi are served with a selection of sauces including pesto, pomodoro, and gorgonzola.

11 ounces Yukon potatoes
1 egg
½ teaspoon salt
Pinch ground nutmeg
¼ teaspoon white pepper
1½ cups all-purpose flour
6 quarts water
½ tablespoon salt
Olive oil, as needed
Pesto sauce, as needed (see page 109)
½ cup parmesan cheese

Wash the potatoes, wrap in aluminum foil, and place on a baking sheet. Bake in a preheated 350 degree F oven for 1½ hours. When done, remove from oven and let cool. Remove potato skins and grind the potato in a potato ricer (or Cuisinart with mixing blade attachment) until mashed. Transfer the mashed potato to a mixer or leave in Cuisinart and add the egg, salt, nutmeg, pepper, and flour. Mix until the potato mixture becomes a ball.

Remove ball from Cuisinart and divide into three sections. Roll each section into long ½-inch rope-like strands. Cut the strands into ½-inch pieces, creating the gnocchi.

Next, cook the gnocchi by boiling 6 quarts of water with the salt. Carefully drop the gnocchi in batches into the boiling water and let water return to a rapid boil. Cook uncovered, stirring occasionally. When done gnocchi will float to the surface after about 5 minutes. Remove from heat, drain, and toss with a little olive oil to avoid the gnocchi sticking together.

In a large sauté pan over medium heat, add the prepared pesto sauce to warm. Add the cooked gnocchi and toss with the pesto. Add half the parmesan cheese and mix well. Transfer to individual serving plates and top with the remaining cheese. Serve immediately.

Chef's note: Gnocchi is the Italian name for dumplings made with flour and potato. Gnocchi can be frozen after cooking, before adding the sauce. Be sure to toss the gnocchi in olive oil and place in a ziplock bag before freezing.

Additional note: To make *Gnocchi al Pomodoro*, simply substitute fresh tomato sauce (see page 103). To make *Gnocchi al Gorgonzola*, substitute gorgonzola sauce for pesto. To prepare the gorgonzola sauce, combine 3½ cups heavy whipping cream, 3 tablespoons crumbled gorgonzola, and ½ teaspoon salt in a large sauté pan over medium heat. Cook for 4 to 5 minutes until sauce reduces. Add the 1½ pounds of gnocchi and toss well with ½ cup parmesan cheese. Serve on individual plates and top with another ½ cup parmesan cheese.

GNOCCHI AGLI SCAMPI
GNOCCHI IN SHRIMP SAUCE
Serves 4

GNOCCHI:
Prepare and cook as on page 137.

SHRIMP SAUCE:
2 tablespoons extra virgin olive oil
2 garlic cloves, smashed
1 to 1½ pounds fresh shrimp, cleaned, shelled and deveined
½ teaspoon salt
¼ teaspoon crushed red pepper
½ cup dry white wine
2 cups heavy whipping cream
½ cup fresh fish stock (see page 79)
2 cups fresh tomato sauce (see page 103)
¼ teaspoon fresh Italian parsley, finely chopped

After preparing the gnocchi, add the olive oil to a large sauté pan over medium-high heat. When hot, add the garlic and sauté until soft and golden brown. Add the shrimp, salt, and red pepper and cook about 2 minutes until shrimp turn color. Add the white wine and cook for several minutes until wine is reduced. Remove the shrimp and add the cream, fish stock, and tomato sauce to the pan. Reduce heat to low and cook for about 4 minutes.

Add the cooked gnocchi to the sauce and toss well. Let cook for about 3 minutes. Add the shrimp back to the pan and mix together. Discard the garlic, and transfer to individual plates. Serve immediately with a sprinkle of Italian parsley on top.

RISOTTO AL ROSMARINO
RISOTTO WITH FRESH ROSEMARY

Serves 4

RISOTTO:

2 tablespoons extra virgin olive oil

3 tablespoons finely chopped yellow onion

1 cup arborio rice

1 cup dry white wine

4 cups chicken stock, gently boiling

½ cup veal stock, gently boiling (optional, or as garnish)

ROSEMARY:

¼ teaspoon chopped fresh rosemary

1 cup fresh grated parmesan cheese, divided

3 tablespoons butter (optional)

In a large sauce pan or small stock pot over medium-high heat, add the olive oil. When hot, add the onions and sauté until soft and golden. Reduce the heat to low and add the rice, stirring constantly, about 2 minutes. Raise the heat to medium, add the white wine, and continue stirring constantly until alcohol evaporates. Add 2 cups boiling chicken stock, stirring for about 10 minutes. Add the remaining 2 cups of boiling chicken stock little by little while stirring (so rice can absorb the stock). At this time, add the veal stock, if desired. This process of adding stock and stirring should take about 15 to 20 minutes.

When the rice is tender, add the rosemary, ½ cup parmesan cheese, and butter if desired. Mix well. Transfer to individual plates and top each portion with a ladle of veal stock and remaining parmesan cheese. Serve immediately.

AS FOR US, FROM THE BIRTHDAYS IN THE BACK ROOM TO THE EMBRACES OF FRANCESCO, THE PHILOSOPHICAL TEACHINGS OF ANTONIO, THE GOOD CHEER OF ROBERTO, MAS, AND MARIO. THE 1000'S OF LAUGHS, THE *VONGOLE*, THE *BURRATA*, THE RIBEYE, THE BOYS PARKING CARS; JUST THE SIMPLE MOMENTS WHEN WE HAVE WALKED IN OUT OF THE RAIN TO SEE THE SMILES, TO FEEL THE CAMARADERIE ... IT IS TRUE THERE IS NO PLACE LIKE HOME AND *TOSCANA* IS OUR HOME.

LOVE, THE ABRAHAMS

RISOTTO ALLA CATALANA
RISOTTO WITH FRESH SHRIMP & SAFFRON

Serves 4

RISOTTO:

Prepare the risotto as directed on page 142 to the point where rice is tender.

SHRIMP & SAFFRON:

2 tablespoons extra virgin olive oil
2 garlic cloves, smashed
1 pound fresh shrimp, cleaned, shelled and deveined
¼ teaspoon salt
splash of white wine
¼ teaspoon saffron threads
¼ teaspoon crushed red pepper
1 teaspoon fresh Italian parsley, finely chopped

After preparing the risotto, add the olive oil to a large sauté pan over medium-high heat. When hot, add the garlic and sauté until soft and golden brown. Add the shrimp, salt, 1 tablespoon of white wine, saffron, and crushed red pepper. Discard the garlic, add the rice to the contents of the seafood pan and mix well. Transfer to individual plates and top with the Italian parsley and a drizzle of extra virgin olive oil.

Chef's note: Do not use more saffron than noted as this spice is extremely strong in flavor.

I HAVE ALWAYS LOVED THE RISOTTO *CATALANA* AND NOW MY SON ORDERS IT TOO. SO YOU NOW HAVE A SECOND GENERATION OF LOYAL CUSTOMERS!

JAVIER ARANGO

RISOTTO PRIMAVERA
RISOTTO WITH FRESH MIXED VEGETABLES
Serves 4

RISOTTO:
Prepare the risotto as directed on page 142 to the point where rice is tender.

MIXED VEGETABLES:
2 cups small diced mixed vegetables (carrot, celery, peas, white mushroom, zucchini)
3 cups fresh tomato sauce (see page 103)
1 cup fresh grated parmesan cheese, divided
3 tablespoons butter (optional)

After preparing the risotto, sauté the vegetables for about 8 to 10 minutes and add them along with the tomato sauce to the risotto. Cook for 4 to 5 minutes. Add ½ cup parmesan cheese and butter, if desired. Mix well. Transfer to individual plates and top with the remaining parmesan cheese. Serve immediately.

Chef's note: For *Risotto alla Paesana*, simply refer to the recipe above, and add 2½ ounces of mild Italian sausage (about 1 link) sliced into four pieces and cooked until brown.

RISOTTO ALLA LIVORNESE
RISOTTO WITH FRESH SEAFOOD
Serves 4

RISOTTO:

Prepare the risotto as directed on page 142 to the point where rice is tender.

SEAFOOD:

4 tablespoons extra virgin olive oil
2 garlic cloves, smashed
10 ounces live Manila clams
8 live New Zealand green mussels
8 ounces fresh shrimp, cleaned, shelled and deveined
8 ounces fresh calamari, tubes and tentacles, cleaned and tubes split in half
1 tablespoon dry white wine
½ teaspoon salt
¼ teaspoon crushed red pepper
2 cups fresh tomato sauce (see page 103)
¼ tablespoon fresh chopped Italian parsley
Extra virgin olive oil, as needed

After preparing the risotto, add the olive oil to a large sauté pan over medium-high heat, add the olive oil. When hot, add the garlic and saute until soft and golden brown. Add the clams, mussels, shrimp and *calamari*, white wine, salt, red pepper, and tomato sauce. Cook for about 2 minutes on high heat, stirring occasionally, until sauce is reduced.

Discard the garlic, and add the tender rice to the seafood pan and let reduce for another 3 to 4 minutes, stirring occasionally. Sprinkle in the Italian parsley and add a drizzle of extra virgin olive oil. Remove from heat, mix well, transfer to individual plates, and serve immediately.

RISOTTO ALLA MILANESE

RISOTTO WITH SAFFRON

Serves 4

RISOTTO:

*Prepare the risotto as directed on page 142 to the
      point where rice is tender.*

VEAL & SAFFRON:

½ cup veal stock
¼ teaspoon chopped fresh rosemary
¼ teaspoon saffron threads
1 cup fresh grated parmesan cheese, divided
3 tablespoons butter (optional)

After preparing the risotto, add the veal stock, rosemary, saffron, ½ cup parmesan cheese,
and the butter if desired. Mix well and transfer to individual plates. Top with the remaining parmesan cheese and serve immediately.

RISOTTO CON LE QUAGLIE
RISOTTO WITH QUAIL
Serves 4

RISOTTO:
Prepare the risotto as directed on page 142 to the point where rice is tender.

QUAIL:
3 tablespoons extra virgin olive oil
4 whole quail
½ teaspoon salt
¼ teaspoon black pepper
2 garlic cloves, finely chopped
¼ teaspoon fresh chopped rosemary
1 chopped fresh carrot
2 stalks chopped fresh celery
½ cup dry white wine
1 cup fresh grated parmesan cheese
3 tablespoons butter (optional)

After preparing the risotto, add 3 tablespoons olive oil to a large sauté pan over medium-high heat. Coat the quail inside and out with salt, pepper, garlic, and rosemary. When oil is hot, add the carrots, celery, and quail, making sure to brown the quail on all sides. Add ½ cup white wine and place pan in a preheated 350 degree F oven for 20 minutes. Remove pan from oven and let rest. When quail are cool enough to handle, debone three, removing and chopping all the meat, reserving the fourth for presentation.

When the rice is tender with about 5 minutes more to cook, add the chopped quail meat and vegetables to the pan, along with the parmesan cheese and butter, if desired, and mix well. Transfer to individual plates and quarter the fourth quail and place on top for presentation.

RAVIOLI AL RADICCHIO
SPINACH RAVIOLI WITH RADICCHIO IN A CREAM SAUCE
Serves 4

SPINACH FILLING:

13 ounces fresh spinach
¾ cup parmesan cheese
¼ teaspoon salt

¼ teaspoon ground nutmeg
1 cup fresh ricotta cheese

In a pot of unsalted boiling water add spinach and cook for 3 minutes. Remove from heat and drain. Press spinach between paper towels to remove excess water. Place cooked spinach in a blender or Cuisinart and finely mince. Add the minced spinach to a mixing bowl with the parmesan cheese, salt, nutmeg, and ricotta. Mix until a pasty consistency is achieved. (This is the filling.)

RAVIOLI ASSEMBLY:

32 small wonton skins (8 per serving)
Egg wash (1 egg whisked with a ¼ cup water)

On a lightly floured surface, lay out the wonton skins and place ¾ tablespoon of spinach filling in the center of 1 wonton. Brush the edges of the wonton with the egg wash. Fold over the skin, forming a triangle. Gently form the wonton around the filling while pressing down to remove all the air and seal the edges of the ravioli. Using a knife or pizza cutter, trim the corners so the ravioli resembles a pentagon. Repeat the steps for the remaining ravioli.

COOKING THE RAVIOLI:

6 quarts boiling water
1 tablespoon extra virgin olive oil
1 cup fresh radicchio, chopped

3 cups heavy whipping cream
1 cup grated parmesan cheese
1 tablespoon butter (optional)

Place the ravioli in a pot of boiling salted water for about 5 minutes, or until the ravioli float to the surface. Remove from heat, drain and set aside.

Meanwhile in a large sauté pan over medium heat, add the olive oil and salt. When oil is hot add the *radicchio* and sauté until brown on the edges. Add the cream and let reduce, about 3 minutes. Add the cooked ravioli and gently swirl the pan to coat the ravioli, about 2 minutes. Sprinkle the parmesan cheese on top. Transfer to individual plates and serve immediately.

RAVIOLI DI ZUCCA
RAVIOLI WITH PUMPKIN IN A PUMPKIN SAUCE
Serves 4

PUMPKIN FILLING:

1 large section of fresh pumpkin (about 1 pound)
½ cup of chopped boiled potatoes
¼ teaspoon salt
¼ cup fresh ricotta cheese
1 egg
3 tablespoons crushed amaretto cookies, plus 1 tablespoon for garnish
¼ cup grated parmesan cheese, plus 1 tablespoon for garnish

Preheat the oven to 350 degree F. Place the pumpkin on a baking sheet, put in the oven and bake for 1 ½ hours until tender. Remove from heat and let cool. When cool, remove the skin and seeds and transfer pumpkin flesh to a Cuisinart. Add the salt, ricotta, egg, cookies, and parmesan cheese. Blend until well combined. (This is the filling.)

RAVIOLI ASSEMBLY:

Assemble ravioli as directed on page 149

COOKING THE RAVIOLI:

6 quarts of boiling water	*4 tablespoons butter*
1 tablespoon extra virgin olive oil	*½ cup vegetable stock*
¼ cup fresh diced pumpkin	*1 tablespoon grated parmesan cheese*
¼ teaspoon fresh thyme	*1 tablespoon crushed amaretto cookie*

Place the ravioli in a pot of boiling salted water and cook for about 5 minutes, or until the ravioli float to the surface. Remove from heat, drain and set aside.

Meanwhile in a large sauté pan over medium heat add the olive oil. When hot add the pumpkin and sauté for about 10 minutes. Add the thyme and butter and continue to cook until butter is melted. Add the vegetable stock and continue to cook until pumpkin is soft and tender, about 3 minutes. Add the cooked ravioli and gently swirl the pan to coat the ravioli, about 2 minutes. Transfer to individual serving plates and top with parmesan cheese and crumbled amaretto cookie.

RAVIOLI DI PORCINI
CON BURRO E SALVIA
RAVIOLI WITH PORCINI MUSHROOM
IN A BUTTER & SAGE SAUCE

Serves 4

PORCINI FILLING:

½ cup carrot, chopped

1 cup celery, chopped

2 tablespoons extra virgin olive oil

1 tablespoon minced yellow onion

¼ garlic clove, smashed

1 teaspoon salt

¼ teaspoon black pepper

2 fresh basil leaves

6 ounces fresh porcini mushrooms, finely chopped

¼ cup white wine

½ cup fresh ricotta cheese

½ egg

⅛ teaspoon nutmeg

¼ cup fresh grated parmesan cheese

In a Cuisinart blend the carrot and celery until finely minced. In a large sauté pan over medium heat add 1 tablespoon extra virgin olive oil. When hot add the onion and garlic and sauté until onions are translucent. Add the minced carrot, celery, salt, pepper, basil, and porcini mushrooms. Stir the vegetables quickly while adding the white wine. Let cook for 5 to 7 minutes until wine is fully reduced. Remove from heat and let cool. When cool add the ricotta cheese, egg, and nutmeg and stir well to combine. Add the remaining tablespoon of olive oil and ¼ cup parmesan cheese. Mix well and add additional salt to taste. (This is the filling.)

RAVIOLI ASSEMBLY:

Assemble ravioli as directed on page 149.

COOKING THE RAVIOLI:

6 quarts of boiling water

3 tablespoons unsalted butter

4 fresh sage leaves

¼ cup fresh grated parmesan cheese plus 2 tablespoons, for garnish

Place the ravioli in a pot of boiling salted water for about 5 minutes, or until the ravioli float to the surface. Remove from heat, drain, and set aside.

Meanwhile in a large sauté pan over medium heat add the butter. When the butter is melted add the sage leaves. Mix in the ravioli and gently swirl the pan to coat the ravioli and let cook about 2 minutes. Sprinkle the ¼ cup parmesan cheese on top and transfer to individual plates. Garnish with extra cheese if desired.

RAVIOLI DI VITELLO

RAVIOLI WITH VEAL, PORCINI MUSHROOMS, & BLACK TRUFFLES

Serves 4

VEAL FILLING:

2 tablespoons extra virgin olive oil, divided

2 tablespoons chopped yellow onion

1 carrot, chopped into 1-inch pieces

2 stalks celery, chopped into 1 inch pieces

¼ teaspoon chopped fresh rosemary

4 ounces fresh veal, cut into 1-inch cubes

½ teaspoon salt

¼ teaspoon black pepper

½ cup dry, white wine

4 cups chicken stock, divided

1 egg

⅛ teaspoon ground nutmeg

½ cup fresh ricotta cheese

¼ cup grated fresh parmesan cheese

Heat a large sauce pan over medium heat and add 1 tablespoon of olive oil. When hot add the onions, carrot, celery, and rosemary and sauté, stirring occasionally until onions are translucent, about 5 minutes. Add the veal, salt, and pepper and brown the veal on all sides. Add in the white wine and continue to stir occasionally. Cook for about 7 minutes to allow the veal to absorb the wine. Stir in 2 cups of the chicken stock. Remove from heat and place the pan in a preheated 350 degrees F oven for 45 minutes. Check every 15 minutes and add the remaining chicken stock as the veal continues to absorb the liquid.

Remove from the oven and let cool. When cool, blend the veal and contents from the pan in a Cuisinart. Transfer the blended veal to a mixing bowl and add the egg, nutmeg, and ricotta cheese. Mix with hands until well incorporated. Add the remaining tablespoon of olive oil and the parmesan cheese and mix again until combined. (This is the filling.)

RAVIOLI ASSEMBLY:

Assemble ravioli as directed on page 149.

COOKING THE RAVIOLI:

6 quarts boiling water

1 tablespoon extra virgin olive oil

10 ounces fresh porcini mushrooms, thinly sliced

½ teaspoon salt

¼ teaspoon black pepper

garlic clove, smashed

1 tablespoon dry, white wine

3/4 cup chicken stock

2 ounces butter (optional)

Splash of truffle oil

¼ cup Parmesan cheese

1 tablespoon shaved black truffle

Place the ravioli in a pot of boiling salted water for about 5 minutes, or until the ravioli float to the surface. Remove from heat, drain and set aside.

Heat 1 tablespoon of olive oil in a large sauté pan over medium heat. When hot add the porcini mushrooms, salt, pepper, garlic, and white wine. When wine is reduced add the chicken stock and butter if desired. Add in the cooked ravioli and gently swirl the pan to coat the ravioli, about 2 minutes. Discard the garlic and transfer ravioli to individual plates and top with a light splash of truffle oil, the parmesan cheese, and shaved black truffle.

Chef's note: Black truffle, although not as revered as the famed white truffle, is readily available in gourmet and specialty food markets

RAVIOLI AL POMODORO
SPINACH RAVIOLI WITH FRESH TOMATO SAUCE
Serves 4

SPINACH FILLING:
For spinach filling recipe see page 149.

RAVIOLI ASSEMBLY:
Assemble ravioli as directed on page 149.

COOKING THE RAVIOLI:
6 quarts boiling water
4 cups fresh tomato sauce (see page 103)
1 cup fresh grated parmesan cheese
1 tablespoon butter (optional)
4 fresh whole basil leaves, for garnish

Place the ravioli in a pot of boiling salted water for about 5 minutes, or until the ravioli float to the surface. Remove from heat and drain.

Heat the tomato sauce in a large sauté pan and add the butter, if desired. When warm add the cooked ravioli and gently swirl the pan to coat the ravioli, about 3 minutes. Sprinkle the parmesan cheese on top and transfer to individual serving bowls. Garnish each bowl with a basil leaf and serve immediately.

Ah, truffles! Truffles are an exotic delicacy featured at *Toscana* throughout the year. However, it is the earthly fragrant white truffle that commands the most attention. Dug up or unearthed in the damp, woody terrain of Alba with the help of dogs and pigs, these culinary gems are carted to Italy's coveted truffle auctions to be obtained by the highest bidder. The white truffle, averaging more than three thousand dollars for a single truffle, is acquired by *Toscana* only during the October through December season. "We purchase the large truffles, which we find much firmer and exude that intoxicating truffle aroma," explains Chef Hugo. For about $100 a serving, guests at *Toscana* can experience truffle bliss by adding a generous shaving of fresh white truffle to any dish, although the most common requests seem to be the *pizza al tartufo* (white truffle pizza) or the heavenly *risotto al tartufo* (white truffle risotto).

PIETANZE COL TARTUFO

Missed the white truffle season? Do not worry, because *Toscana* offers other delectable truffles to satisfy truffle aficionados. The black truffle, commonly collected in the Pacific Northwest of the United States, France, and Italy, makes its restaurant debut in the spring and lingers through the year. Enjoy paper-thin slices of black truffle over tender white asparagus or atop a bed of creamy risotto with fresh *porcini* mushrooms. When the weather heats up in Southern California, look for summer truffles to appear in such savory *Toscana* dishes as fresh day-boat scallops with *cannellini* beans or tucked inside handmade ravioli. When purchasing truffles for home use, Chef Hugo recommends wrapping them in a dry paper towel and storing the truffles on a bed of uncooked rice inside a sealed container in the refrigerator. This will keep the truffles fresh while retaining their full aroma and flavor. "But don't hoard them," the chef says. White truffles only last about one week, while black and summer truffles can store for about 15 days.

ASPARAGI AL TARTUFO
ASPARAGUS WITH WHITE TRUFFLE
Serves 1

6 spears fresh white asparagus
1 tablespoon melted butter
1 tablespoon fresh grated parmesan cheese
¼ teaspoon truffle oil
½ ounce fresh shaved white truffle
¼ vine-ripe tomato, diced for garnish
¼ teaspoon fresh chopped Italian parsley, for garnish

Peel the asparagus and boil in water for 5 to 7 minutes until tender. Remove from heat, drain, and arrange in the center of a single serving dish. Drizzle the melted butter, parmesan cheese, and truffle oil on top of the asparagus. Top with the fresh shaved white truffle and garnish with diced tomato and parsley.

KUDOS TO MIKE GORDON, WHO FOR 20 YEARS HAS BROUGHT THE "BEST" OF ITALY TO BRENTWOOD.

ROD AND SANDY CHASE

PIZZA AL TARTUFO
FRESH WHITE TRUFFLE PIZZA

Makes 1 (10-to 12-inch) pizza

1 (7 ounce) ball fresh pizza dough (see page 89)
3 ounces shredded mozzarella cheese
½ ounce fresh shaved white truffle
¼ teaspoon truffle oil

Dust a smooth working surface with flour. Place one pizza dough ball in the center. Flatten the dough into a disc shape with fingers. Next, roll the dough with a rolling pin until the dough is thin and reaches a diameter of 10 to 12 inches. Sprinkle generously with mozzarella cheese. Using a metal or wood peel, place the pizza in a wood-fired oven, away from the fire, and let bake for several minutes.

After baking several minutes, turn the pizza 180 degrees and continue baking for another few minutes or until crust is golden brown and the cheese is bubbly. Remove pizza from the oven. Arrange the shavings of fresh white truffle on top. Finish with a drizzle of truffle oil.

If using a conventional oven, preheat the oven with a pizza stone positioned on the middle rack for 30 minutes at 500 degrees F. When heated place the pizza directly on the stone. Bake for approximately 6 minutes.

THERE HAVE BEEN SO MANY MEMORIES OF BEING TREATED SO WARMLY, WITH DEEP AFFECTION AND REGARD BY YOUR STAFF—THAT OUR FONDEST MEMORIES COULD FILL A COOKBOOK ON THEIR OWN!

SUSAN AND JERRY LEIDER

RISOTTO AL TARTUFO

RISOTTO WITH WHITE TRUFFLE

Serves 4

2 tablespoons extra virgin olive oil
3 tablespoons finely chopped yellow onion
5 ounces arborio rice
1 cup dry white wine
4 cups chicken stock, divided
¼ teaspoon fresh chopped rosemary
1 cup fresh grated parmesan cheese, divided
3 tablespoons butter (optional)
¼ teaspoon truffle oil
½ ounce fresh shaved white truffle

In a large sauce pan over medium-high heat, add the olive oil. When hot, add the onions and sauté until translucent. Reduce the heat to low and add the rice, continuously stirring for about 2 minutes. Raise the heat to medium and add the white wine, stirring constantly until reduced. When the liquid begins to boil, add 2 cups chicken stock and stir. Add the remaining 2 cups of chicken stock little by little while stirring. This process of adding stock and stirring should take about 15 minutes.

When the rice is tender, add the rosemary, ½ cup parmesan cheese, and butter if desired. Mix well. Transfer to individual serving plates and top with the remaining parmesan cheese, truffle oil, and fresh shaved white truffles. Serve immediately.

FILETTO DI BUFALO AL TARTUFO NERO
BUFFALO FILET WITH BLACK OR SUMMER TRUFFLES

Serves 4

4 (8 ounce) buffalo steaks
4 ounces pancetta, thinly sliced into 4 pieces
2 tablespoons extra virgin olive oil
¼ teaspoon salt
¼ teaspoon black pepper
¼ cup dry white wine
2 tablespoons heavy whipping cream
4 tablespoons butter
¼ cup chicken stock
¼ teaspoon truffle oil
12 slices fresh black or summer truffle

Preheat oven to 450 degrees F. Wrap one slice of pancetta around each buffalo steak, using a toothpick to secure. Heat the olive oil in a large sauté pan over medium-high heat. When hot, add the steaks and cook 3 minutes on each side. Add the salt, pepper, and white wine, and let reduce, about 3 minutes.

Place pan with steaks in oven for approximately 8 minutes for medium rare. Remove from oven and set meat aside. Into the pan add the cream, butter, and a little chicken stock if necessary. Add in the truffle oil and stir until well combined. Place each steak on an individual serving dish. Top each with the sauce and fresh slices of summer truffles.

TAGLIATELLE AL TARTUFO
FETTUCCINE WITH WHITE TRUFFLE

Serves 4

1 pound tagliatelle pasta
6 quarts water
1 tablespoon salt
5 tablespoons fresh grated parmesan cheese, divided
¼ teaspoon truffle oil
2 tablespoons butter (optional)
½ ounce fresh shaved white truffle

Prepare the pasta by boiling 6 quarts of water with 1 tablespoon of salt. Add the pasta and stir, returning to a rapid boil. Cook uncovered according to package directions until al dente, stirring occasionally. When done, remove from heat, drain and transfer the cooked pasta to a large sauté pan.

Add half the parmesan cheese, truffle oil, and butter, if desired. Mix well. Transfer to individual serving plates and top with the remaining cheese and fresh shaved white truffle. Serve immediately.

IT ALWAYS FEELS LIKE HOME AND THE FOOD IS ALWAYS PERFECT.

STEVEN GORDON

Fresh, wild and hearty are perfect adjectives to describe the tender meats and moist, flakey fish that the kitchen prepares night in and night out. At *Toscana*, Chef Hugo and his culinary team rule the grill and considerable portions are always guaranteed, especially *la fiorentina*. The trattoria's signature T-bone is a hefty 26-ounce USDA prime grass-fed steak, custom cut for the restaurant. "This steak is as fat as a text book and really defines us," says co-owner Andy Gordon, an avowed carnivore himself. The juicy T-bone, like much of the sumptuous meat and seafood dishes served at the restaurant, is quickly seared,

CARNE E POLLO
E PESCE

finished in *Toscana's* glowing wood-fired oven, and stamped with its own crosshatches from the oven's grill. Whether it's the veal *milanese*—never dry and so simple yet flavorful—the *branzino*, or the *pollo mattone*, every sizzling entree is deliciously moist, tender, and loaded with flavor. *Toscana* always selects the finest cuts of beef and poultry, and the freshest fish. Alaskan halibut, Lake Superior whitefish, John Dory from New Zealand, and market squid delivered fresh from the fertile Pacific Ocean, are just some of the seafood specialities available at *Toscana*, each guaranteed to satisfy the most discerning palate.

MEDAGLIONI DI MANZO CON FUNGHI
FILET MIGNON WITH PORCINI MUSHROOMS

Serves 2

Toscana only selects prime grass-fed, dry-aged beef.

2 (10 ounce) prime filet mignon medallions
1 tablespoon olive oil
½ teaspoon extra virgin olive oil
Salt, as needed
Black pepper, as needed
1 garlic clove, smashed
4 ounces fresh porcini mushrooms, sliced (7 ounces if frozen)

Coat the filet mignons with salt, black pepper, and regular olive oil. Grill each filet over a hot flame or outdoor grill, about 5 minutes per side for medium-rare. Remove from heat and let rest.

In a sauté pan over medium-high heat, add the extra virgin olive oil. When hot, add the garlic and sauté until soft and golden brown. Add the *porcini* mushrooms, ½ teaspoon of salt, and sauté for about 5 to 6 minutes. Discard the garlic.

Transfer the filet mignons to individual serving dishes and top with the mushrooms and pan juices. Serve with a side of spinach (see page 216) and roasted potatoes (see page 217).

TOSCANA IS . . . FRANCESCO'S WARM, WONDERFUL EMBRACE, ANTONIO'S WELCOMING SMILE, THE MOST ATTENTIVE STAFF AND MAGIC IN THE KITCHEN.

ELLEN & RICHARD SANDLER

BRASATO AL BAROLO
SHORT RIBS WITH RED WINE

Serves 4

5 tablespoons extra virgin olive oil
2 pounds boneless beef short ribs
¼ teaspoon chopped garlic
¼ teaspoon fresh chopped rosemary
¼ teaspoon fresh chopped sage
½ cup chopped carrot
2 cups chopped celery
2 cups chopped yellow onion
2 ⅓ cups Italian red wine
9 cups water
6 cups fresh tomato sauce (see page 103)
1 teaspoon salt
½ teaspoon black pepper

In a large sauce pan or medium-size stock pot over medium-high heat, add the olive oil. When hot, add the short ribs and sear each side for about 5 minutes. Remove the ribs and add the garlic, rosemary, and sage, stirring for 2 minutes. Add the chopped carrot, celery, and onion, and sauté for 5 minutes.

Return the ribs to the pan and add the wine. Reduce heat to medium and let simmer for 15 minutes. Add the water, tomato sauce, salt, and pepper, and stir until blended. Remove from heat. Place sauce pan or pot in a preheated 300 degrees F oven (uncovered) for 3 hours. When meat is tender and falling off bone, remove from oven and serve over mashed potatoes or polenta (see page 220).

OUR FAMILY GOES TO TOSCANA FOR ROSH HASHANA, YOM KIPPUR, AND WHENEVER WE WANT TO JUST HAVE A MEAL THAT BRINGS US CLOSER TO GOD. IN MY CASE, THE *BRASATO* ALWAYS DOES THE TRICK.

ROBERT & JENNY MORTON

FIORENTINA

TOSCANA'S SIGNATURE CUT T-BONE WITH SPINACH & POTATOES

Serves 4

2 (26 ounce) T-bone steaks
2 tablespoons extra virgin olive oil
½ teaspoon salt
¼ teaspoon black pepper
Extra virgin olive oil, as needed

Season the T-bones with the 2 tablespoons of olive oil, salt, and pepper. On a hot outdoor barbecue or stove top grill, sear the steaks for 4 minutes on each side. Remove from heat and finish the steaks in a preheated 500 degrees F oven for about 15 minutes, for medium rare. Remove from oven and let rest for 5 minutes.

Arrange the steaks on individual serving plates. Serve with a side of potatoes (page 217) and spinach (page 216). Finish with a drizzle of flavorful olive oil.

Chef's note: T-bone steaks are cut from the front end of the short loin and contain a smaller section of the tenderloin. A porterhouse is a similar T-bone cut, but made from the rear end of the short loin.

TAGLIATA ALLA TOSCANA CON RUCOLA
SLICED RIBEYE OVER ARUGULA
Serves 4

2 pounds prime ribeye (bone-out)
¼ teaspoon salt
¼ teaspoon black pepper
1 tablespoon extra virgin olive oil
4 cups fresh arugula
Drizzle of extra virgin olive oil
12 ounces shaved parmesan cheese

Season the ribeye with the olive oil, salt, and pepper. On a hot kitchen grill or outdoor barbecue, grill the ribeye about 7 minutes each side to sear. Remove ribeye from heat and finish in a preheated 350 degrees F oven for 15 minutes, for medium rare. Remove from heat and let rest, about 5 minutes.

Plate the arugula on a large platter. Slice the ribeye into thin uniform slices and arrange on top of the arugula. Drizzle the slices with extra virgin olive oil and top with the shaved parmesan cheese.

STRACCETTI DI MANZO
THE TAIL OF FILET MIGNON
WITH SUN-DRIED TOMATO

Serves 4

4 tablespoons extra virgin olive oil
½ teaspoon finely chopped garlic
1 ½ pounds prime filet mignon, thinly sliced
5 ounces sun-dried tomatoes, julienne
1 teaspoon salt
1 teaspoon black pepper
1 teaspoon fresh rosemary
4 cups fresh spinach
12 ounces fresh shaved parmesan cheese

Heat a large sauté pan with the olive oil. When hot, add the garlic and sauté until lightly golden. Add the sliced filet mignon, sun-dried tomatoes, salt, pepper, and rosemary. Sauté for 3 minutes, stirring occasionally. Raise the heat to high and add the spinach, tossing well. Remove from heat and transfer to individual serving dishes. Top with the parmesan cheese shavings.

Chef's note: Toscana uses the highest quality beef, and always prepares *Straccetti* with filet mignon. Feel free to use other cuts of beef as an alternative to filet mignon. Also, this is a very quick dinner that can be prepared within minutes.

GREAT LOCATION. GREAT FOOD. WONDERFUL STAFF. ALL TO BE CELEBRATED. FRANCESCO IS A MAESTRO! *GRAZIE.*

GIL FRIESEN

STINCO DI AGNELLO

BRAISED LAMB SHANKS

Serves 4

4 tablespoons extra virgin olive oil
4 (14 to 16 ounces) fresh lamb shanks
2 or 3 carrots, diced
3 stalks celery, diced
½ yellow onion, diced
½ teaspoon fresh thyme
1 cup dry white wine
7 cups water
3 cups fresh tomato sauce (see page 103)
½ teaspoon salt
¼ teaspoon black pepper

In a large sauce pan or medium-size stock pot over medium-high heat, add the olive oil. When hot, add the lamb shanks and sear each side for about 5 minutes.

Remove the shanks and add the chopped carrots, celery, onion, and thyme, and sauté for 5 to 7 minutes.

Return the lamb shanks to the pan and add the wine. Reduce heat to medium and let simmer for 15 minutes. Add the water, tomato sauce, salt, and pepper, and remove from heat. Place sauce pan or pot in a preheated 300 degrees F oven (uncovered) for 2 hours 15 minutes. When cooked, remove from oven and serve over polenta (see page 220).

BISTECCA CON FAGIOLI
BONE-IN RIBEYE WITH CANNELLINI BEANS
Serves 4

4 (20 ounce) bone-in ribeye steaks
2 tablespoons plus ½ teaspoon extra virgin olive oil
½ teaspoon salt
¼ teaspoon black pepper
½ teaspoon extra virgin olive oil
1 garlic clove, smashed
½ cup white cannellini beans (see page 53 for cooking instructions)
½ teaspoon red wine vinegar
Pinch of fresh Italian parsley, finely chopped
Extra virgin olive oil, as needed

Season the ribeyes with 2 tablespoons of olive oil, salt and pepper. On a hot outdoor barbecue grill, sear the steaks for 4 minutes on each side. Remove from heat and finish the steaks in a preheated 500 degrees F oven for about 15 minutes, for medium rare. Remove from oven and let rest for 5 minutes.

In a separate sauté pan add ½ teaspoon of olive oil, the smashed garlic clove, cooked white *cannellini* beans and red wine vinegar. Cook over medium-high heat for several minutes, remove and discard the garlic. Next, arrange the steaks on individual serving plates. Serve with a side of cooked *cannellini* beans, a pinch of Italian parsley, and a drizzle of olive oil.

CARRÉ D'AGNELLO
BABY LAMB RACK
Serves 1

10 ounces New Zealand baby lamb rack, about 6 pieces
¼ teaspoon salt
¼ teaspoon black pepper
1 tablespoon plus ½ teaspoon extra virgin olive oil
¼ teaspoon fresh chopped rosemary
1 garlic clove, smashed
2 tablespoons veal glaze

Coat the lamb rack with the salt, pepper, 1 tablespoon olive oil, and rosemary. Over a hot kitchen grill, or outdoor barbeque, grill the lamb rack about 5 minutes per side for medium-rare. Remove from heat and let rest.

In a sauté pan over medium-high heat, add the ½ teaspoon extra virgin olive oil. When hot, add the garlic and sauté until soft and golden brown. Add the lamb rack and sauté with the veal glaze for 2 minutes. (Note: If the sauce is too watery, add ½ teaspoon of butter.)

Remove from heat, discard the garlic, and slice the rack between each bone (about 6 pieces). Transfer to an individual serving dish, pour the juices from the pan over the lamb, and serve with a side of spinach (see page 216) and roasted potatoes (see page 217).

Chef's note: Veal glaze can be purchased in most markets and specialty food shops.

WHEN WE THINK ABOUT *TOSCANA* WE THINK ABOUT ALBERTO. WE HAVE KNOWN HIM FOR 30 YEARS AND SHARED MANY BOTTLES OF WINE WITH HIM.

JEFF AND ADELE GAULT

OSSOBUCO
BRAISED VEAL SHANKS
Serves 4

4 tablespoons extra virgin olive oil
4 (14 to 16 ounces) fresh veal shanks
2-3 carrots, chopped
3 stalks celery, chopped
½ yellow onion, chopped
½ teaspoon fresh thyme
1 cup dry white wine
7 cups water
3 cups fresh tomato sauce (see page 103)
½ teaspoon salt
¼ teaspoon black pepper

In a large sauce pan or medium-size stock pot over medium-high heat, add the olive oil. When hot, add the veal shanks and sear each side for about 5 minutes.

Remove the shanks and add the chopped carrots, celery, onion, and thyme, and sauté for 5 to 7 minutes.

Return the veal shanks to the pan and add the wine. Reduce heat to medium and let simmer for 15 minutes. Add the water, tomato sauce, salt, and pepper, and remove from heat. Place sauce pan or pot in a preheated 300 degrees F oven (uncovered) for 2 hours 15 minutes. When cooked, remove from oven and serve over *Risotto alla Milanese* (see page 146).

YOUR WONDERFUL STAFF HAS MADE ME FEEL AT HOME FOR THE LAST 20 YEARS. THEY HAVE FED ME, MADE ME LAUGH, AND FRANKLY, EVEN THOUGH THEY RIPPED OFF POT ROAST FROM THE JEWS, I STILL LOVE THEM.

DAN RISSNER

COSTOLETTA ALLA MILANESE
BREADED VEAL CHOP

Serves 1

12 ounce veal chop (with bone)
2 eggs
1 tablespoon milk
¼ teaspoon salt
¼ teaspoon black pepper
½ cup dried breadcrumbs
2 cups vegetable oil

Prepare the veal chop by trimming all the fat. Then place the chop between two sheets of plastic wrap. Using a kitchen mallet, pound the chop until ¼-inch thick. If the bone gets in the way or is too long, simply remove excess.

In a large mixing bowl, whisk together the eggs, milk, salt, and pepper. Lay out the breadcrumbs on a large plate. Next, dredge the veal chop in the egg and milk mixture and then dredge in the breadcrumbs. Place the chop between the two sheets of plastic wrap and again lightly pound with the kitchen mallet to help secure the breadcrumbs to the chop.

In a large cast iron skillet, heat the vegetable oil over high heat. When hot, carefully deep-fry the chop about 4 minutes per side, until golden brown. Remove chop from the oil and drain on paper towel. Transfer to an individual serving dish and serve with a side of fresh arugula, spinach (see page 216), and chopped tomato (see page 220).

DURING MY THREE PREGNANCIES THERE WERE THREE DIFFERENT FAVORITE DISHES—SPAGHETTI *POMODORO* WHEN I WAS PREGNANT WITH DAVID. VEAL *MILANESE* WITH ALISON, AND THE SEAFOOD RISOTTO WITH EMILY.

JEFF AND STEPHANIE JACOBS FAMILY

SPEZZATINO DI VITELLO

VEAL STEW

Serves 4

6 tablespoons olive oil
2 pounds fresh veal shoulder, cut into large cubes
2-3 carrots chopped
1 cup chopped celery
1 cup chopped yellow onion
2 garlic cloves, crushed
4 ounces fresh porcini mushrooms (or 7 ounces frozen)
½ cup fresh green peas (or frozen)
1 teaspoon salt
½ teaspoon black pepper
½ teaspoon fresh thyme
2 cups dry white wine
8 cups water
1 ½ pounds Yukon potatoes, cut into 6 to 8 large cubes

In a large sauce pan or medium-size stock pot over medium-high heat, add the olive oil. When hot, add the veal and sear the meat for about 5 minutes each side.

Remove the meat and add the chopped carrots, celery, onion, garlic, *porcini* mushrooms, peas, salt, pepper, and thyme. Reduce heat to medium and sauté for 7 to 8 minutes, stirring occasionally.

Return the veal to the pan and add the wine. Let simmer for 4 to 5 minutes so wine can reduce. Add the water and continue to simmer another 5 minutes. Add the potatoes, stir to blend all ingredients well, and simmer for an additional 20 minutes, or until potatoes are tender. Transfer to individual serving bowls and serve with a side dish of spinach (see page 216).

NODINO DI VITELLO
BONE-IN VEAL CHOP

Serves 1

14 ounce bone-in veal chop
¼ teaspoon salt
¼ teaspoon black pepper
1 tablespoon extra virgin olive oil
1 tablespoon butter
4 fresh sage leaves, 2 reserved for garnish

Coat the veal chop with the salt, pepper, and olive oil. Over a hot flame on an indoor grill or outdoor barbeque, grill the veal, about 5 minutes per side for medium-rare. Remove from heat and let rest.

In a sauté pan over medium-high heat, melt the butter with 2 sage leaves. When melted, add the veal chop to the pan and toss to coat. Remove from the pan and transfer to a serving plate. Pour the juices from the pan over the veal, and garnish with a couple fresh sage leaves. Serve with a side of spinach (see page 216) and roasted potatoes (see page 217).

I AM A PARTICULAR FAN OF YOUR GRILLED VEAL CHOP, AND WE LOVE WATCHING ALBERTO DRINK OUR WINE! FRANCESCO MAKES US FEEL LIKE FAMILY AND, WEEK IN AND WEEK OUT, *TOSCANA* IS OUR FAVORITE RESTAURANT.

STEVEN & DAYNA BOCHCO

POLLO AL MATTONE
CHICKEN WITH ROSEMARY & SAGE
COOKED UNDER A "BRICK"

Serves 4

2 whole chickens (about 3 pounds each), cleaned and butterflied with breast bones removed
2 tablespoons extra virgin olive oil
¼ teaspoon salt
¼ teaspoon black pepper
1 teaspoon chopped fresh sage leaves
1 tablespoon chopped fresh rosemary
1 garlic clove, smashed
½ cup dry white wine

Prepare chickens by rubbing each chicken with ½ tablespoon olive oil, salt, pepper, sage, and rosemary. On a hot kitchen grill or outdoor barbecue, grill the chicken for about 7 minutes on each side.

Remove from grill and place chickens (skin side up) in a deep roasting pan. Add the garlic, white wine, and remaining tablespoon of oil. Place pan in a preheated 350 degrees F oven for 45 minutes. Remove from heat, section each chicken into 6 pieces and plate. Pour the pan juices over the chicken and serve with a side of spinach (see page 216) and potatoes (see page 217).

Chef's note: This is a very traditional dish served in Tuscany, and a popular dish at *Toscana*, featured on the original menu. *Mattone* in Italian means brick, which is placed on top of the chicken to flatten while cooking.

PETTO DI POLLO CON CARCIOFI

CHICKEN WITH ARTICHOKES

Serves 4

ARTICHOKES:

6 pounds baby artichokes
Cold water (about 1 gallon)
¼ cup fresh lemon juice
1 tablespoon extra virgin olive oil
1 garlic clove, smashed
1 teaspoon salt
1 teaspoon black pepper
½ cup white wine

CHICKEN:

4 chicken breasts, boneless and skinless
1 cup all-purpose flour
4 tablespoons extra virgin olive oil
¼ teaspoon salt
¼ teaspoon black pepper
¼ cup dry white wine
1 cup chicken stock
4 tablespoons butter

Prepare artichokes by removing the tough outer leaves. Slice each artichoke into 4 pieces and transfer to a large bowl filled with very cold water and lemon juice. Allow artichokes to soak for no less than one hour.

In a large sauté pan over medium-high heat, add the olive oil. When hot, add the garlic and sauté until garlic is lightly golden. Drain the artichokes and add them to the pan, along with the salt and pepper, stir to combine. Raise the heat to high and continue to cook for about 5 minutes, stirring occasionally. Add the white wine and cook for an additional 7 minutes, or until wine has reduced. Remove from heat.

Next, prepare the chicken by butterflying each breast. Dredge each breast in the flour. Heat a large sauté pan with the extra virgin olive oil over medium-high heat. When hot, add the chicken along with salt and pepper. When golden brown, flip the chicken and cook the other side. When the underside is golden brown, add the white wine and let reduce, about 5 minutes. Lower the heat to medium and add the cooked artichokes, along with the chicken stock. Continue to cook for 5 minutes, or until stock has reduced. Stir in the butter, and remove from heat. Arrange chicken breasts on individual plates and pour sauce and artichokes on top. Serve with spinach (see page 216) and roasted potatoes (see page 217).

POLLO ALLA CACCIATORA
CHICKEN CACCIATORA

Serves 4

2 whole chickens (about 3 pounds each), cleaned and sectioned
1 teaspoon salt
1 teaspoon black pepper
1 cup all-purpose flour
4 tablespoons extra virgin olive oil
1 garlic clove, smashed
½ medium-size onion, chopped
¼ cup kalamata olives, pitted
7 ounces fresh porcini mushrooms
1 pound fresh Roma tomatoes, quartered
1 cup dry white wine
1 cup chicken stock
1 teaspoon fresh rosemary

Wash the chicken pieces and pat dry. Then prepare the chicken by rubbing with salt and pepper. Dredge each piece in flour and shake off excess. Heat the olive oil in a large sauté pan over medium heat. When hot, add the chicken pieces and cook until golden brown, about 4 minutes each side.

Remove the chicken from the pan, and add the garlic, onions, olives, mushrooms, and tomatoes. Sauté for 5 minutes, stirring occasionally. Add the white wine and cook for about 3 minutes. Add the chicken stock and allow liquid to reduce, about 10 minutes.

Return the chicken to the pan (do not move the chicken once it is placed), and add the rosemary. Reduce the heat to low, and let cook for 30 to 35 minutes. Remove from heat, plate chicken, and top with the pan juices and vegetables. Serve with a side of spinach (see page 216) and polenta (see page 220).

PAILLARD DI POLLO
POUNDED CHICKEN WITH ROSEMARY

Serves 4

4 chicken breasts, boneless and skinless
1 tablespoon extra virgin olive oil
½ teaspoon salt
¼ teaspoon black pepper
¼ teaspoon chopped fresh rosemary

Prepare the chicken by butterflying each breast. Place each breast between two pieces of plastic wrap and using a kitchen mallet pound the breast until thin (about ¼-inch). Coat each breast with olive oil, salt, pepper, and rosemary.

On a hot kitchen grill or outdoor barbecue, grill the chicken breasts about 4 minutes each side, until golden brown and cooked through. Transfer the chicken breasts to individual serving dishes, along with a side of spinach (see page 216) and roasted potatoes (see page 217).

SALMONE AL VAPORE CON RUCOLA
SALMON WITH ARUGULA

Serves 4

1 stalk celery, chopped
1 carrot, chopped
4 sprigs fresh Italian parsley, whole
4 (8 ounce) fresh Alaskan wild-caught salmon filets
4 cups fresh arugula
2 fresh vine-ripe tomatos, sliced
2 tablespoons extra virgin olive oil

Add the celery, carrot, and parsley to a large pot of salted water. Boil water over high heat. When water is boiling, add the salmon and boil for 7 minutes. Remove salmon.

Divide the arugula between individual serving dishes and arrange the slices of tomato along the edges. Place one piece of salmon on top of each mound of arugula. Finish with a drizzle of extra virgin olive oil.

Chef's note: When boiling or steaming seafood, add vegetables such as celery, carrots, and parsley to the water for added flavor.

WE LOVE COMING HERE EVERY WEEK BECAUSE YOU'RE THE CLOSEST THING TO ITALY! TOSCANA IS A HOME AWAY FROM HOME.

THE WARSAVSKY FAMILY

BRANZINO INTERO
ITALIAN STRIPED BASS
Serves 4

*4 whole stripped bass (approximately 1½ pounds each), wild or farm-raised,
    cleaned and gutted with head intact*
2 tablespoons extra virgin olive oil
½ teaspoon salt
¼ teaspoon black pepper

Coat the bass, inside and out, with the olive oil, salt, and pepper. On a hot kitchen grill or outdoor barbecue, grill the fish about 4 minutes per side. Remove from heat and place fish in a preheated 450 degrees F oven for 8 minutes, until moist and flakey. Remove from oven and plate on individual serving dishes. Serve with a side of spinach (see page 216) and chopped tomato (see page 220).

Chef's note: At *Toscana*, whole fish are deboned and plated table-side. At home, filets can be used as an alternative to whole fish if bones are of concern.

PESCE SPADA ALLA GRIGLIA

SWORDFISH

Serves 4

4 (8 ounce) fresh swordfish steaks
2 tablespoons extra virgin olive oil
½ teaspoon salt
¼ teaspoon black pepper
1 fresh lemon, juiced
¼ teaspoon finely chopped fresh Italian parsley
Drizzle of extra virgin olive oil

Coat the swordfish with the olive oil, salt, and pepper. On a hot kitchen grill or outdoor barbecue, grill the fish about 4 minutes per side.

Remove from heat and plate on individual serving dishes. Top with fresh lemon juice, parsley, and a drizzle of extra virgin olive oil. Serve with a side of spinach (see page 216) and chopped tomato (see page 220).

IT'S LIKE OUR KITCHEN AWAY FROM HOME. WE EVEN HOST OUR COMPANY CHRISTMAS DINNER PARTY IN THE BEAUTIFUL WINE CELLAR. WE LOVE THE ITALIAN FLAIR.

RENZO, IRENE, AND ILONA CASELLINI

SOGLIOLA
DOVER SOLE
Serves 4

4 whole fresh dover sole (approximately 1 pound each),
*   cleaned and gutted with head intact*
2 tablespoons extra virgin olive oil
½ teaspoon salt
¼ teaspoon black pepper

Coat the sole, inside and out, with the olive oil, salt, and pepper. On a hot kitchen grill or outdoor barbecue, grill the fish about 5 minutes per side.

Remove from heat and place fish in a preheated 450 degrees F oven for 8 minutes, until moist and flakey. Remove from oven and plate on individual serving dishes. Serve with a side of spinach (see page 216) and chopped tomato (see page 220).

TOO MANY MEMORIES OF GOOD FOOD, WINE, AND FRIENDS TO COUNT.

WIDO SCHAEFER

HALIBUT CON POMODORINI
HALIBUT WITH CHERRY TOMATOES
Serves 4

4 (8 ounce) fresh Alaskan halibut filets
2 tablespoons extra virgin olive oil, divided
1 teaspoon salt, divided
½ teaspoon black pepper, divided
1 garlic clove, smashed
1 pound fresh cherry tomatoes, halved
1 tablespoon dry white wine
¼ teaspoon finely chopped fresh Italian parsley
Drizzle of extra virgin olive oil

Coat the halibut with 1 tablespoon olive oil, 1 teaspoon salt, and ½ teaspoon pepper. On a hot kitchen grill or outdoor barbecue, grill the fish about 5 minutes per side. Remove from heat.

In a large sauté pan over medium heat, add the remaining tablespoon of olive oil. When hot, add the garlic and sauté until soft and lightly golden. Add the halibut, along with the remaining salt, pepper, and cherry tomatoes. Continue to cook for 4 minutes, stirring occasionally, until tomatoes have broken down.

Remove from heat, discard the garlic, and transfer to individual serving dishes. Top each halibut filet with the tomato sauce, sprinkle of parsley, and a drizzle of extra virgin olive oil. Serve with a side of spinach (see page 216).

SAN PIETRO IN SALSA DI LIMONE E CAPPERI

JOHN DORY WITH LEMON & CAPERS

Serves 4

4 (8 ounce) fresh John Dory filets, skin removed
2 tablespoons extra virgin olive oil
1 teaspoon salt
1 teaspoon black pepper
2 tablespoons butter
1 tablespoon capers
2 fresh lemons, juiced
1 tablespoon dry white wine
1 teaspoon finely chopped fresh Italian parsley

Coat the John Dory filets with the olive oil, salt, and pepper. On a kitchen grill or outdoor barbecue, grill the filets until light golden brown about 2 minutes per side. Remove from heat.

In a large sauté pan, melt the butter, capers, and lemon juice. Cook for 3 minutes and add the white wine and continue cooking another couple of minutes until wine reduces. Plate the John Dory on individual serving dishes, and top with the butter, lemon, and caper sauce. Top with fresh Italian parsley and serve with spinach (see page 216) and chopped tomato (see page 220).

Chef's note: At *Toscana*, the seafood entrees are light. When selecting what side dishes to accompany fish, choose spinach, chopped tomato, or green beans rather than heavy sides such as potatoes.

PESCE BIANCO ALLA PIZZAIOLA
WHITE FISH

Serves 4

4 (8 ounce) fresh white fish filets
2 tablespoons extra virgin olive oil, divided
¼ teaspoon salt
¼ teaspoon black pepper
2 garlic cloves, smashed
3 tablespoons capers
1 tablespoon dry white wine
3 cups fresh tomato sauce (see page 103)
½ cup fresh fish stock (see page 79), if needed to thin sauce
¼ teaspoon finely chopped fresh Italian parsley

Coat the white fish with 1 tablespoon olive oil, salt and pepper. On a hot kitchen grill or outdoor barbecue, grill the fish about 5 minutes per side. Remove from heat.

In a large sauté pan over medium heat, add the remaining tablespoon of olive oil. When hot, add the garlic and sauté until soft and lightly golden. Add capers and white wine. Continue to cook for 3 minutes. Add the tomato sauce and fish stock if desired, and cook for an additional 4 minutes, stirring occasionally.

Remove from heat, discard the garlic, and transfer to individual serving dishes. Top each white fish filet with the tomato sauce and a sprinkle of parsley. Serve with a side of spinach (see page 216).

Just like pairing a particular wine with a certain food, it is equally important to select the perfect complementary side dish to enhance the main course. At *Toscana*, it's all about the main course, which is why you will discover limited side dishes, but each with its own uncomplicated yet extraordinary flavor. When preparing a dinner for family or friends at home, *Toscana's* Chef Hugo suggests the best complement to your meal is a bowl of fresh sauteed spinach or rosemary roasted potatoes at the table. For an even lighter variation try simple-to-make polenta,

CONTORNI

or substitute strong-flavored vegetables with the fragrant medley of fresh chopped tomato, basil, and extra virgin olive oil—a favorite at most family tables in Italy. Speaking of the family table, co-founder Mike Gordon has a fun little tale to share. "I recall one night Bill Cosby was celebrating his birthday at our Family Table and he received a gift of a beautiful designer Hawaiian shirt. I was seated at the counter observing the gift exchange, and quipped to Mr. Cosby, 'That's a very nice shirt but it would look better on me.' The next day I received a gift box containing a similar shirt signed, 'with love from Bill Cosby.'" Mike now believes wishes do come true *alla tavola della famiglia*.

SPINACI SALTATI
SAUTEED SPINACH

Serves 4

1 pound fresh spinach leaves
1 teaspoon extra virgin olive oil
1 garlic clove, smashed
¼ teaspoon salt
¼ teaspoon black pepper
Drizzle of extra virgin olive oil
Lemon wedge, for garnish

Add the spinach to a medium-size pot of unsalted boiling water. Let cook for exactly 2 minutes. Remove from heat, drain and transfer spinach to an ice bath (bowl filled with cold water and ice) to stop the cooking process. When spinach is cold, drain and squeeze out excess water by pressing spinach between paper towels.

In a medium-size sauté pan over medium-high heat, add the teaspoon of olive oil. When hot, add the garlic and sauté until soft and lightly golden. Add the cooked spinach and toss well with the salt, pepper and drizzle of olive oil. Remove from heat, discard garlic, and serve with a wedge of lemon on the side.

Chef's note: At *Toscana*, sometimes crushed red pepper (also known as *peperoncino*) is added to the spinach for a little bite.

PATATE ARROSTO
ROASTED ROSEMARY POTATOES

Serves 4

4 Yukon potatoes (about 2 pounds)
2 tablespoons chopped yellow onion
1 tablespoon salt
1 tablespoon olive oil
1 teaspoon fresh rosemary

Wash and peel the potatoes. Cut into 1-inch cubes and place into a medium-size pot of boiling water. Add the salt and onions and cook for 10 to 12 minutes. Next, pre-heat a large sauté pan over medium heat with 1 tablespoon olive oil.

Remove potatoes from heat, drain, and transfer boiled potatoes and onions to the pan. Add the rosemary and sauté for several minutes, or until potatoes are golden-brown. Remove from heat and place pan in a pre-heated 350 degrees F oven for 10 minutes. Remove from oven and garnish with a little extra rosemary and another drizzle of olive oil.

TO EAT AT TOSCANA IS TO BE IN *FORTE DEI MARMI*: EXQUISITE FOOD, STAFF THAT TREATS YOU LIKE FAMILY, AND A GENUINE FEELING OF CARE. *BRAVISSIMO!!*

MINTON, BOBBIE, & HARRY RITTER

CIME DI RAPA IN PADELLA

RAPINI

Serves 4

1 pound fresh rapini
1 tablespoon extra virgin olive oil
1 garlic clove, smashed
¼ teaspoon salt
¼ teaspoon black pepper
¼ teaspoon crushed red pepper flakes
Drizzle of extra virgin olive oil
Lemon wedge, for garnish

Add the *rapini* to a medium-size pot of unsalted boiling water. Let cook for 7 minutes. Remove from heat, drain, and transfer rapini to an ice bath (bowl filled with cold water and ice) to stop the cooking process. When *rapini* is cold, drain, and squeeze out some the water (not all) by pressing *rapini* between paper towels.

In a medium-size sauté pan over medium-high heat, add the tablespoon of olive oil. When hot, add the garlic and sauté until soft and lightly golden. Add the cooked *rapini* and toss well with the salt, black pepper, red pepper flakes, and a drizzle of olive oil. Remove from heat, discard garlic and serve with a wedge of lemon on the side.

POLENTA
POLENTA
Serves 4

6 cups chicken or vegetable stock, divided
1 teaspoon salt
1⅓ cups polenta
2 tablespoons extra virgin olive oil
2 tablespoon fresh grated parmesan cheese

In a medium-size pot, boil 4 cups of the chicken or vegetable stock. When boiling, add the salt and polenta, stirring rapidly so polenta doesn't stick. Cook for about 4 minutes. Add remaining 2 cups of stock a little at a time while stirring. Cook for 6 minutes or until all the liquid has absorbed. Add the olive oil and parmesan cheese. Mix well, remove from heat and serve.

POMODORI CON BASILICO "CHECCA"
CHOPPED TOMATO AND BASIL
Serves 4

4 fresh vine-ripe tomatoes, finely chopped
6 to 8 fresh basil leaves, finely chopped
¼ teaspoon salt
¼ teaspoon black pepper
1 tablespoon extra virgin olive oil

In a bowl combine the chopped tomato, basil, salt, pepper, and olive oil. Toss well to combine and serve.

Ambience, service, and food are three key components that make an enjoyable meal. At *Toscana*, the ambience is cozy and delightful, the service impeccable, and the award-winning courses are faultless, with perfect temperature, flavor, and presentation. This isn't more true than *Toscana's* decadent desserts. In addition to the melt-in-your-mouth *tiramisu* crafted without liquor and the sinfully delicious chocolate tart, there are options like fresh ricotta cheese cake and *torta della nonna* as well as a kaleidoscope of fresh fruit tarts. "We use the absolute best products, but in a simple yet innovative way," says *Toscana's* Chef Hugo, who remains as devoted to his everyday diners as to the

DOLCI

first-timers who stop in for an unexpected meal of a lifetime. Perfectly layered banana tarts, plump blueberry tarts, and artfully designed fruit tarts garner the most attention, and are very easy to make at home. "It is important to use whatever fruit is in season," affirms the pastry chef, who never compromises freshness. Most diners believe the best treat is *Toscana's* signature star cookies—simple, light, flaky pastry dough dusted with powdered sugar, folded in the shape of a star, and baked until golden brown. Served alongside a cappuccino or by themselves, the *stelline* cookies are always available and displayed near the door, and always sought after, whether coming or going. These marvelous cookies further represent friendship, family, and sincere gratitude for dining at Brentwood's premiere Tuscan trattoria.

PASTA FROLLA
ITALIAN PASTRY DOUGH
Makes 3 (15 ounce) dough crusts

8 ounces unsalted butter, softened
4 ounces sugar
2 eggs
5 cups pastry flour
½ lemon zest
½ teaspoon yeast

In a mixing bowl, whisk the butter and sugar until well combined. Add the eggs, flour, lemon zest and yeast. Whisk until a ball is formed. Remove from bowl and divide into 3 balls of approximately 15 ounces each. Let rest at room temperature for 10 to 15 minutes. Extra dough can be frozen for later use.

Chef's note: For perfect rising desserts, *Toscana* uses the Italian yeast *Lievito Pane degli Angeli*. It can be ordered online or found at Italian specialty stores.

CREMA PASTICCIERA
PASTRY CREAM

2½ cups milk
8 egg yolks
½ cup sugar
½ teaspoon vanilla extract
1½ cups flour

In a pot over medium-high heat, boil the milk. Remove from heat and set aside. In the top of a double broiler whisk the egg yolks, sugar, and vanilla until combined. Whisk in the flour a little at a time, until incorporated. With the flame low, slowly whisk in the boiled milk until the pastry cream is formed.

CROSTATA DI FRUTTA
FRUIT TART

Serves 6

1 (15 ounce) pasta frolla (see page 225).
1 cup heavy whipping cream
2½ teaspoons sugar
¼ teaspoon vanilla extract
Fresh fruit (strawberry, kiwi, blackberries, etc., about 12 ounces total), thinly sliced

Roll out one pasta *frolla* and fit inside the bottom and sides of a 10-inch greased tart pan. Trim the edge with a knife, removing the excess dough. Poke the dough with a fork before baking the tart shell in a preheated 350 degrees F oven for 15 minutes. Remove from the oven and let cool. When cool, carefully remove the shell from the pan and transfer to a large serving plate.

Next, in a mixing bowl, whisk the cream, sugar, and vanilla together until stiff peaks form. Spread the whipped cream inside the tart, filling the shell. Arrange the fresh fruit slices on top of the cream, forming the top layer. Use all strawberries, all blackberries, or a variety of fruits.

CROSTATA DI BANANA

BANANA TART

Serves 6

1 (15 ounce) pasta frolla (see page 225).
1 cup heavy whipping cream
2½ teaspoons sugar
¼ teaspoon vanilla extract
2½ bananas (about 12 ounces total), thinly sliced on the diagonal
2 tablespoons cocoa powder

Roll out one pasta *frolla* and fit inside the bottom and sides of a 10-inch greased tart pan. Trim the edge with a knife, removing the excess dough. Poke the dough with a fork before baking the tart shell in a preheated 350 degrees F oven for 15 minutes. Remove from the oven and let cool. When cool, carefully remove the shell from the pan and transfer to a large serving plate.

Next, in a mixing bowl, whisk the cream, sugar, and vanilla together until stiff peaks form. Spread the whipped cream inside the tart, filling the shell. Arrange the banana slices in a circular pattern, working from the outside edge into the center on top of the cream, forming the top layer. Dust the top with cocoa powder and serve.

CROSTATA DI MIRTILLI
BLUEBERRY TART
Serves 6

1 pound fresh blueberries
3 tablespoons sugar
¼ teaspoon vanilla extract
1 (15 ounce) pasta frolla (see page 225).
Egg wash (1 egg whisked with 1 tablespoon water)
Confectioners sugar

In a mixing bowl, lightly mash the blueberries. Add the sugar and vanilla, and mix well until combined. Next, roll out one pasta *frolla* and fit inside the bottom and sides of a 10-inch greased tart pan. Trim the edge with a knife, removing the excess dough. Add the blueberry filling and smooth the top with a knife.

Using the excess dough, roll out into a 10-inch rectangle and slice with a knife into ½-inch strips, approximately 12 to 14. Crisscross the strips on top of the tart. Brush the strips with the egg wash.

Bake the tart in a preheated 350 degrees F oven for 30 minutes. Remove from the oven and dust with confectioners sugar before serving.

DINING AT TOSCANA IS LIKE COMING HOME... A WARM GREETING AT THE DOOR, YUMMY HOMECOOKED FOOD, GOOD WINE, AND GOOD CONVERSATION. WHO SAYS YOU CAN'T GO HOME AGAIN?

THE NANCY & GARY FREEDMAN FAMILY

TORTA AL CIOCCOLATO BIANCO
WHITE CHOCOLATE TART

Serves 6

1 (15 ounce) pasta frolla (see page 225).
5 ounces melted bitter sweet chocolate
5 ounces crema pasticciera (see page 226)
5 ounces whip cream (see Chef's note, below)
2 ounces shaved white chocolate

Roll out one pasta *frolla* and fit inside the bottom and sides of a 10-inch greased tart pan. Trim the edge with a knife, removing the excess dough. Poke the dough with a fork before baking the tart shell in a preheated 350 degree F oven for 15 minutes. Meanwhile melt the chocolate in a double boiler. When *frolla* is done, remove from the oven and let cool. When cool, carefully remove the shell from the pan and transfer to a large serving plate.

Then in a mixing bowl, mix the *crema pasticciera* with the melted chocolate. Transfer the chocolate cream to the tart, filling half the shell. Add the whip cream to fill the remaining half. Top generously with shavings of white chocolate, forming a third layer.

Chef's note: To make fresh whip cream, whisk approximately 1 cup heavy whipping cream, 2½ teaspoons powdered sugar, and ¼ teaspoon vanilla extract in a mixing bowl until stiff peaks form. The cream is now ready for use.

TORTA AL CIOCCOLATO

CHOCOLATE TART

Serves 6

16 ounces bittersweet chocolate, chopped into pieces
3 egg whites
½ cup milk
¼ teaspoon vanilla extract
1 tablespoon sugar
1 (15 ounce) pasta frolla (see page 225)
Confectioners sugar

In a double boiler, melt the chocolate. When melted, add the egg whites and whisk until combined. Add the milk, vanilla, and sugar, and continue whisking until incorporated. Remove from heat.

Next, roll out one pasta *frolla* and fit inside the bottom and sides of a 10-inch greased tart pan. Trim the edge with a knife, removing the excess dough. Add the chocolate filling and smooth the top with a knife. Bake the tart in a preheated 350 degrees F oven for 35 minutes. Remove from the oven and dust with confectioners sugar before serving.

Chef's note: A double boiler consists of two fitted saucepans. A large saucepan is partially filled with water and brought to a boil. A smaller saucepan is placed inside the larger pan so the indirect heat can melt the chocolate.

TORTA DI NOCI

NUT TART

Serves 6

2 teaspoons sugar

⅔ cup whole almonds, shelled

⅔ cup pine nuts

¾ cup amaretto cookies

¼ teaspoon Italian yeast (see page 225 for Chef's note)

¼ teaspoon vanilla extract

½ cup milk

½ teaspoon honey

2 eggs

1 (15 ounce) pasta frolla (see page 225)

In a Cuisinart, blend the sugar, almonds, pine nuts, amaretto cookies, and yeast. Add the vanilla, milk, honey, and eggs and continue to blend until incorporated.

Next, roll out one pasta *frolla* and fit inside the bottom and sides of a 10-inch greased tart pan. Trim the edge with a knife, removing the excess dough. Fill the tart shell with the nut and amaretto cookie mixture, smoothing the top with a knife.

Bake the tart in a preheated 350 degrees F oven for 35 minutes. Let cool and serve.

WHEREVER WE ARE IN THE WORLD, WE DREAM OF YOUR *TORTA DI NOCI.*

KATE GANZ & DANIEL BELIN

TORTA DELLA NONNA

GRANDMOTHER'S CAKE

Serves 6

1 (15 ounce) pasta frolla (see page 225)
16 ounces crema pasticciera (see page 226)
5 ounces shaved milk chocolate
½ cup sliced almonds
Confectioners sugar

Roll out one pasta *frolla* and fit inside the bottom and sides of a 10-inch greased tart pan Trim the edge with a knife, removing the excess dough. Add the *crema pasticciera* to the center of the tart shell. Arrange the shavings of milk chocolate on top of the cream.

Using a knife, trim the excess dough around the edges, and roll to form a second sheet. Place the second sheet of dough over the top of the cream and chocolate and seal the edges. Stick the almonds into the top sheet of dough by piercing the almonds halfway through.

Trim all excess dough if any, and bake in a preheated 350 degrees F oven for 30 minutes. Remove from the oven and dust with confectioners sugar before serving.

TORTA DI RICOTTA
RICOTTA CHEESE CAKE
Serves 6

10 ounces cream cheese, softened
3 tablespoons sugar
½ teaspoon vanilla extract
¼ cup milk
13 ounces fresh ricotta cheese, drained
2 eggs
1 (15 ounce) pasta frolla (see page 225).
Confectioners sugar

In a Cuisinart, blend the cream cheese, sugar, vanilla extract, milk, and ricotta cheese. Add the eggs and continue to blend until incorporated.

Next, roll out one pasta *frolla* and fit inside the bottom and sides of a 10-inch greased tart pan. Trim the edge with a knife, removing the excess dough. Add the ricotta cheese filling and smooth the top with a knife.

Bake the tart in a preheated 350 degrees F oven for 35 minutes. Remove from the oven and dust with confectioners sugar before serving.

TIRAMISU

Serves 4

3 jumbo eggs, separated
⅓ cup granulated sugar
1 teaspoon vanilla
1 lb mascarpone cheese
2 cups espresso
24 pcs lady fingers
1 cup grated dark chocolate

Combine the 3 egg yolks and sugar in a mixer using the whisk attachment. Whisk until well blended and creamy, about 5 minutes. Then add the teaspoon of vanilla and the *mascarpone* cheese and beat altogether for about 8 to 10 minutes until the mixture is completely blended.

In another bowl whip the egg whites into soft peaks. Add egg whites to the *mascarpone* mixture and mix gently until well combined. In a small gratine or serving dish, spread a layer of the *mascarpone*. Pre-soak about 8 of the ladyfingers in the espresso and layer on top of the *mascarpone*. Spread another layer of *mascarpone* on top of the ladyfingers and pre-soak another 8 ladyfingers, and layer on top of the *mascarpone* as before. Repeat, creating 3 layers. Finally, generously sprinkle the grated dark chocolate on top. Refrigerate for 1 hour before serving.

STELLINE

TOSCANA STAR COOKIES

Makes about 12 cookies

1 (12 ounce) French puff pastry dough sheet, rolled out to approx. 9 x 12 inches
Granulated sugar, as needed
Egg wash (1 egg whisked with 1 tablespoon water)
Powdered sugar, as needed

Defrost one sheet of French puff pastry dough. Spread the granulated sugar on both sides of the dough. Using a pizza cutter or sharp knife, divide the granulated sugar dough into 15 equal squares. Next, slice each corner of the dough square stopping just short of the center. Put a drop of egg wash on center of each square, and with the fingers, fold the right corners and pinch them in the center, forming a star.

Transfer the stars to a greased baking sheet and bake them in a preheated 350 degrees F oven for 40 minutes, or until golden brown. Let cool, sprinkle generously with powdered sugar and serve.

Chef's note: Since making homemade pastry dough takes considerable time, try using pre-made puff pastry dough. It is very quick and equally delicious.

ACKNOWLEDGEMENTS

Kathie and Mike and Amy and Andy Gordon
wish to say thank you to the members of our *famiglia*
without whom *Toscana* nor this 20th anniversary cookbook would exist.

Doc Severinsen — besides being an award-winning musician and a great friend, Doc was the visionary and inspiration behind the creation of *Toscana*.

Agostino Sciandri — although he departed many years ago, Agostino was our first Executive Chef and creator of many of the items on our menu.

Francesco Greco — the exciting leader of our *famiglia del Toscana*. He is a respected and charismatic General Manager and Managing Partner who is unofficially known as the Mayor of Brentwood. Along with his smile and hugs, he has taken *Toscana* to greater financial success and customer enjoyment.

Hugo Cruz Vasquez — our newest Executive Chef, Hugo has taken *Toscana's* menu to a new level of creativity and excellence. Chef Hugo has been with us from the very beginning and adds a certain calm to the kitchen which, along with his food, soothes and nurtures us all.

Antonio De Cicco — our dashing and athletic maitre d' assists Francesco in ways too numerous to mention. Antonio brings just the right touch of Italian charm that adds warmth to everyone's experience with us.

Alberto Pais — our consummate head waiter whose "restaurant within a restaurant" enjoys the affections of Hollywood's most famous.

Mark Galasso — Italian in heritage, he is the most senior and cherished member of our wait staff. Mark is adored by all our clients, their children and now, their children's children.

Roberto Facciolla — a real "can-do" waiter. He is the maestro in the private dining room making sure every party guest goes home happy… and full!

Massimo DeMori, Max Valentino, and Roberto Savorani – round out our team of professional waiters who cater to our customers' whims and create the hum within the dining room.

Antonella Greco – the mother hen who succeeds in controlling the chaos and is the rock of our staff. When we need the job done we give it to this woman.

Gabrielle Semoni and Maria Moraru – our warm and beautiful hostesses who make you want to come back.

Talia Tinari, Wine Director – a knowledgable guide who has been a help in implementing our award-winning wine program.

Piero Topputo – a former Executive Chef.

Zenon Martinez, Florencio Perez, Miguel Luis Martinez, Filiberto Mateo, Jesus Gutierrez, Humberto Vasquez, Ramiro Jimenez, Justino Quirino, Isauro Santiago, Michael Vega and Victor Cruz – our brilliant, hard-working chefs and cooks, who add strength and support to Chef Hugo, and keep the food amazingly delicious.

Juan Tirado and Antonio Luis Tobias – our ever-loyal, diligent kitchen preps who help keep our cooks cooking.

Jesse Flores, Pedro Ruiz Molina, Ricardo Mota, Abel Lopez, Miguel Mateo, Saul Aguilar, Martin Gonzales, Isaias Hernandez, and Porfiorio Garcia – a team of indefatigable bussers who keep life simple for everyone in the restaurant.

Eric Major – Kathie's son and probably our most loyal and versatile employee. His eagle-CPA's eye keeps us in the black.

Kenny Kerr – our accountant and "*fagioli*"-counter.

Carol Zuckerman – Andy's mother and the inspiration behind our authentic Italian décor.

Joan Luther — our publicist who early on helped put us on the world map.

Matt and Moonie Fishburn — Mike's partner and his wife, the givers of the "Puck gift" whose patience and support enabled Mike to pursue his dream.

Gabriel and Jorge Silva — our loyal and trusted valet team who have been with us since the beginning. Not even a scratch in 20 years!

***the*BookDesigners** — bright young stars who put together our beautifully designed book.

Jessica Nicosia-Nadler — a professional food photographer in every sense of the word. Her work truly amazes and inspires.

Meagan Szasz — an incredibly talented, lifestyle photographer who captured the heart and soul of *Toscana* through her lens.

James O. Fraioli — an extremely talented, multi award-winning author whom we first met on a bocce court in Santa Ynez. Familiar with his amazing cookbooks, we spoke to him about helping us to create our own cookbook for *Toscana*. He surpassed our every expectation.

A special note from Kathie & Mike to all our children — all five of you who have made food your passion too; you will never know the depth of the pleasure we have had of cooking together, sharing meals, and enjoying good times — at *Toscana* and home.

And last but definitely not least:

Our Loyal Customers — without whom we would be just another Italian restaurant.

Grazie Mille!

INDEX

LA FAMIGLIA DEL
TOSCANA